空手道

A. PFLUGER

*Black Belt, 2nd Dan,
Japan Karate Association*

KARATE

BASIC PRINCIPLES

BARNES & NOBLE, INC.
NEW YORK
PUBLISHERS • BOOKSELLERS • SINCE 1873

Copyright © 1967
by Sterling Publishing Co., Inc.
419 Park Avenue South, New York, N. Y. 10016

All rights reserved

Translated by
Dale S. Cunningham and Paul Kuttner
From the German edition published by
Falken-Verlag Erich Sicker, Wiesbaden

Reprinted 1972 by Barnes & Noble, Inc.
through special arrangement with
Sterling Publishing Co., Inc.

L.C. Catalog Card Number: 75-118104

SBN 389 00313 1

Printed in the United States of America

Contents

The Technique of Karate

"Karate, an art of fighting that originated in China, uses all of the limbs of the body for defence and attack." This statement tells in a few words the essence of a competitive sport from the Orient, a sport that is extremely varied and is becoming increasingly well known.

Karate (pronounced "kah-rah-teh"), in reality, is not as simple and uncomplicated as this statement. On the contrary, every Karate teacher finds again and again that his beginning students lose perspective and begin to despair because of the many techniques they must learn. In this book will be offered some new methods and aids, especially for the teacher. Certain mechanical and psychological laws are important to know before you can understand the technique of Karate. It is also possible for the student himself to understand the technique of Karate once he achieves the correct point of view.

By study, you will discover similarities and relationships again and again between various techniques. Eventually the technique of Karate as a whole will then no longer appear to be a collection of various techniques. Once a person understands the entire technique of Karate, he gets a complete "overview," and the whole area no longer seems large and difficult to survey. Moreover, any technique of Karate which was not known to you before, no longer seems to be completely "new." You understand it because it is subject to the same principles that you have already been working to understand. Therefore, the first prerequisite for learning Karate is *correct understanding*.

Practice is useful only after you understand the technique of Karate being demonstrated. The prerequisite for understanding is *exact observation* of the technique being demonstrated or exact reading of the instruction book. This brings up another very important point. Understanding a technique alone is not sufficient. You must be able to make the technique your very own, and this comes through *practice*.

It can very well happen that someone has understood a technique, practices it all the time, and in spite of this, does not

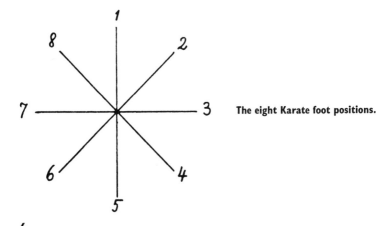

The eight Karate foot positions.

succeed in mastering perfect technique. *Self-criticism* or critical self-observation is lacking. You know how a technique should look. So, you very critically observe yourself doing it. You improve on it, work on it. You look critically again and again. How is *kokutsu-dachi* (the back stance) supposed to look, and how does it look when I do it? You have to compare and see what is wrong with your performance and then correct it. By practicing this way, with understanding and self-criticism, you have a great advantage over the person who practices, say, three hours every day, but has not understood the techniques and does not know what he is doing wrong.

For that reason, the phrase "less is more," when correctly understood, is valid for Karate. Ten jabs with the fist every day practiced with understanding and self-criticism (in front of a mirror) can be more valuable than hours of thrusting back and forth like a robot while understanding is lacking.

No one can promise that you will master Karate in a short time. But that is no excuse for not practicing with understanding and self-criticism, and then practicing again and again.

In summing up, here are the prerequisites for learning Karate:
1. Exact observation and concentration.
2. Understanding.
3. Practice, while
4. Observing yourself critically.

These are the prerequisites for learning the *technique* of Karate. However, Karate does not consist only of technique. The second part of this book treats the philosophical side in great detail, but in this first part we are concerned with technique alone.

Body tension

Karate is a competitive sport in which the concentrated force of your body is pressed for a short moment at some point of your opponent's body for the purpose of defence or attack. Expressed in another way, it is control of the tension of your body at the right moment—the muscles are tensed only for a short moment, the moment of striking, then are immediately relaxed again. Your body at the moment of striking stands there behind the technique as hard as a block of granite.

The tenser the muscles of your body are during this short moment, the better. During this extremely short instant, there must be no weak spot in your body. The technique must be perfected while the "substructure" is solid. The peaks of tension in position and in striking must occur simultaneously for the techniques to have a great shock effect.

You must be able to move swiftly and gracefully in Karate, and fast graceful movements are possible only when you are relaxed. Therefore, the tensing must be only a very short term thing. However, it is the decisive thing in Karate, for without it Karate would be just an acrobatic dance with soft, supple movements.

You have to be able to combine the hard with the soft—a goal that you can achieve only after long years of intensive study. The old Chinese masters laughed at anyone who tried only to introduce

Illus. 1. Normal breathing. It is easy for your partner to lift you up.

Illus. 2. Breathing from the diaphragm. By concentrating on the hara, you will stick to the floor.

strength into his techniques, for a true master combines the soft and the hard. He is neither soft nor hard, but rather both at the same moment. This sentence from a book on gymnastics is valid: "Whoever is master of relaxation (intellectually and spiritually as well) is also master of tension." The key to this ability of being both hard and soft at the same time (and combining them) lies in the *hara*, which can be practiced very consciously. However, more about that later.

The low stance

The lower you stand, the greater the security of your stance, for the surface of your stance is greater and your center of gravity is lowered. The fact of the matter is that your defence or attack technique will be that much more effective the better the security of your stance. In addition, your low stance supplies tension in your bent legs (as in a drawn bow) which you can apply in a flash to attack or withdraw quickly. However, to extract the greatest measure of effectiveness, something else is also important.

The direction of the tension

All positions in Karate are thought out to give them the maximum effect for a particular purpose (whether attack or defence, to the rear or to the side). Expressed differently, the position makes it possible to let the concentrated tension of your body become highly effective during defence and attack in whatever direction is necessary.

The technical significance of "hara"

The literal translation of *hara* means "stomach," but in the figurative sense it indicates the true center of gravity of a person, the very middle. We will discuss the figurative sense of *hara* in detail in the second half of this book. At this point we merely want to discuss its technical meaning very briefly. There is an old Chinese saying, "Before you can learn to conquer others, you must first learn to stand well." Whoever loses his balance is weak. He cannot defend himself or attack effectively. In order to maintain your equilibrium, you must concentrate on the center of your body, your center of gravity, your *hara*. Here, in the significance of *hara*, Karate has the same basis as Judo or Aikido.

Whatever the position connected with a technique, the force from the *hara* must be concentrated at one point. Always think consciously of the fact that the strength for every technique comes from the *hara*.

So as not to get your midpoint out of balance, so that all action can start forcefully and effectively from the center of your body, it is important to hold yourself erect. Keep your body in each of your Karate positions and actions so that your navel always points up slightly.

A good exercise of *hara* is breathing with your diaphragm. This type of breathing is practiced consciously by the masters of Judo and especially by practitioners of Aikido. The inhaled air is pressed down, and breathing is done not so much by lifting and releasing the chest as by moving the diaphragm up and down. By breathing this way, you can lower your center of gravity somewhat. This means that although you are standing on the same surface area, the security of your stance is greater.

This is valid to the same extent for Karate, Judo, and Aikido. The significance of the *hara* is that it is the center of gravity and at the same time the center of equilibrium of the body. "Whoever loses his balance cannot bring technique into play and is already half beaten."

Breathing

Correct breathing is more important than anything else in Karate. In Karate you must master body tension, you must concentrate your strength at a certain moment, and in order to obtain the highest measure of effectiveness, you must breathe very consciously.

Inhaling makes relaxation easier; exhaling helps you when tensing. Various systems of gymnastics are based on this fact. As far as Karate is concerned, this means that you exhale at the moment you develop your greatest force, and you do this quickly, like an explosion!

In Karate you often see opponents using force while holding

their breath. Many Judokas also hold their breath at the moment of the greatest development of strength (at the beginning of a throw). However, from a medical viewpoint, this is usually considered unhealthy. In addition, it is not very efficient. We know today, after an extensive series of experiments carried out by sports physicians and physiologists that the greatest force is developed at the point when half the air in the lungs has been expelled. You must have at some time experienced this fact yourself. For example, you may have had to lift a heavy object from the floor to the table. You take hold of it, but it is so heavy you can hardly lift it from the ground. What do you do? You tense all your muscles, you exert yourself and involuntarily you gasp—you inhale deeply, and then you exhale. All of a sudden you can lift it up quickly. In the course of doing this, you exhaled part of the air that you were previously compressing, and in doing this you helped your muscles to tense. This is the main reason for uttering the battle cry of Karate, "KIAI," which helps to attain your maximal body tension at the moment of striking.

The hip is the point of origin of every total movement

The basic principle for every total movement is: Hip first—limbs afterwards.

We will encounter this principle again and again in every technique.

1. Stances and Movements

The positions and movements of Karate differ essentially from those of everyday life. In Karate, your body always moves as a whole with your hip (more exactly, the *hara*) as the center point. Your leg does not proceed and your body follow after, but rather every movement is a unity, originating and determined by the center of gravity and force of the body, the *hara*. The following "tests" will show you whether your movements are suitable for Karate, i.e., whether they start from the *hara*.

Illus. 4 (left). The basic stance, hachiji-dachi, from which you can move easily into one of the low, tensed positions, such as kiba-dachi (below).

Illus. 5a. Kiba-dachi position of the feet and knees.

Illus. 5b. Kiba-dachi stance.

Hachiji-dachi, the basic stance

Body relaxed and natural (Illus. 3 and 4). This stance leaves all possibilities and directions open. From this position, you can slide into one of the low, tensed positions, for example, into *kiba-dachi*.

Kiba-dachi, the straddle-leg stance

This position is particularly strong at the sides. Your feet are spread apart twice the breadth of your shoulders, your toes pointing slightly to the inside. The weight of your body is distributed evenly, and your knees are pressed to the outside (Illus. 5 and 6). In this way, your position becomes solid and contains a great supply of tension. Keep the upper part of your body erect. Breathe with your diaphragm. Push your hips forward.

13

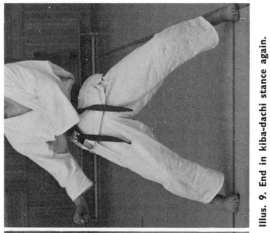

Illus. 9. End in kiba-dachi stance again.

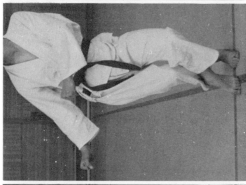

Illus. 8. Legs crossed for a split second.

Illus. 7. Glide from kiba-dachi to left.

Illus. 6. Kiba-dachi.

Cross-over side movement in kiba-dachi

Let's see how you would move sideways from the *kiba-dachi* stance, for example, to your left (Illus. 7 to 9). The important thing is to be relaxed and glide! Do not bend your hips, but bend your supporting (right) leg, and cross your left foot in front of it.

During all movements from this and other Karate positions, imagine that a low ceiling is just above your head. Tense all your muscles briefly at the moment you have spread and placed your right leg down in its final position. Press both knees to the outside at the same time and tense your abdomen (breathing through your diaphragm). By doing this, you will immediately stand sure and solid.

180-degree turn

For a pivot on your left foot, draw up your right foot to cross close behind the left, so that the center of gravity moves along evenly. Only when your right leg touches your supporting (left) leg do you turn your body 180 degrees. Your supporting leg should

Illus. 10

Illus. 11

In the 180-degree turn, you pivot on your left foot, and bring your right foot past it in a straight line.

remain markedly flexed, and this will help fling the other leg far to the side (Illus. 10 and 11). By forcefully turning on your hip, you use the supply of tension in your bent supporting leg, and this makes the movement rapid and full of power. Tense all muscles for a moment and breathe with your abdominal wall abruptly exhaling.

For practice

From the *hachiji-dachi* (basic) stance, go into *kiba-dachi*, then move at a right angle to the front and to the rear, to the left and to the right. Practice sharp turning of your hip and tensing of your abdominal wall.

Here is a little test which will reveal whether you are able already to move in a way suitable for Karate, whether your movements proceed from the *hara* or from the limbs.

Your partner takes a strong stanglehold on your neck from the front (Illus. 12). You draw up your chin, hold your shoulders high, tense your neck muscles. If you now were to take a step to the side (either leg first), it would be an easy matter for him to throw you down in a second (for you would then be standing momentarily on one leg).

16

However, it is possible to escape this hold merely by a true Karate movement into *kiba-dachi*, the straddle-leg stance.

When your opponent has a stranglehold on you, glide back as quick as lightning into a low *kiba-dachi* at right angles. Turn your hip in sharply. Remain erect and tense your abdominal wall. Your opponent will loosen his grip and be pulled off balance (Illus. 13). If you carry out this movement with forceful unity, your opponent will have no opportunity to throw you down. Practice with strong opponents, and don't give up until you can pass this test, even with hefty stranglehold attacks.

Illus. 12   ⸲ Illus. 13

Getting away from a strangle on your neck.

Zenkutsu-dachi, the forward stance

This is an extremely strong front position. It is used in defending against attacks from the front and particularly for attacking and counter-attacking to the front.

17

Illus. 14   **Illus. 15**
The forward stance, zenkutsu-dachi, from which you can defend easily by turning away.

Take a stance with your left foot extended two shoulder breadths forward and out (Illus. 14, 15 and 16). Your front leg carries 60 per cent of your body weight, your rear leg 40 per cent. Your rear leg must be completely extended with your knee straight and your toes pointed as far as possible to the front. Your heels remain flat on the floor.

From side to side, your feet are a shoulder breadth apart, with your front toes turned in slightly.

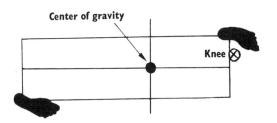

Illus. 16a. The foot and knee positions in zenkutsu-dachi.

From the hachiji-dachi stance (Illus. 17, left) make a small arc with your right foot (Illus. 18, right) as you move forwards into the zenkutsu-dachi.

Your body can now be directed to the front in the *zenkutsu-dachi* stance, or it can be turned away. Particularly in defending, you want to turn away in order to give your opponent as little surface area to attack as possible.

Going into the zenkutsu-dachi stance from hachiji-dachi

Step forward with your right foot, making a small arc from the inside outwards. Let your sole glide close to the floor (Illus. 17 and 18). Remember that your body proceeds as a unit with your hip as the central point. Tense all your muscles momentarily as

Illus. 16b. In the zenkutsu-dachi, your front leg must carry 60 per cent of your body weight.

19

Illus. 19. From the basic hachiji-dachi, glide backwards with your right foot in an arc. Keep your sole parallel to and close to the floor, and leave 60 per cent of your weight on your forward leg.

you place your foot down. Tense your abdominal wall and stand straight.

In stepping backwards with your right foot in an arc from *hachiji-dachi* leave your weight on your front leg. At the same time, bend this supporting leg markedly and shove your left hip to the front (Illus. 19). Your navel must point slightly upwards. Extend your right leg markedly to the rear.

Illus. 20 (left). From the zenkutsu-dachi with left foot forward, you can move in one giant step to zenkutsu-dachi with right foot forward (Illus. 21).

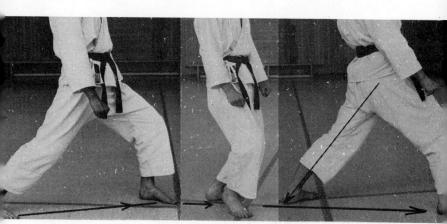

Illus. 22   Illus. 23   Illus. 24
Pass your forward-moving leg very close to your supporting leg and bend low.

If you combine the backward and forward movements of the same leg, you can make a giant step (Illus. 20 and 21 and 22 to 24).

From the rear your right leg goes past your left leg very closely. Keep your supporting leg (left) sharply bent. (Think of the low ceiling over your head!)

The supply of tension in your supporting leg (in this case, the left) enables you to catapult your body correctly to the front. To be sure of accomplishing this, slant your bent supporting leg abruptly forward as soon as your advancing leg has passed the supporting leg. Move your right hip forward. As you place your right leg down, tense all the muscles of your body briefly. Then you will immediately be standing securely and solidly. Proceed continuously in this *zenkutsu-dachi* (forward) stance.

Practice this forward catapulting of your body. You should be conscious of the fact that it is the strength, the supply of tension, in your bent supporting leg which catapults you so rapidly forward. While you are practicing this giant forward step, which you will be using when attacking, think also of your rear leg, which you must *thrust out energetically and forcefully*. Try to speed it forward faster and faster. Always utilize completely the force of

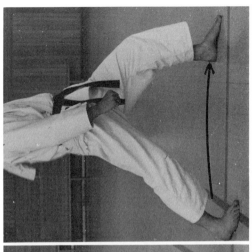

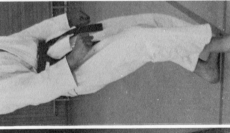

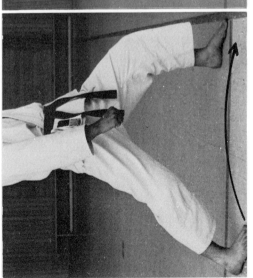

Illus. 25   Illus. 26   Illus. 27

From this giant step forward you start from the zenkutsu-dachi by bringing up your right foot, and in the same forward movement you energetically advance your left foot. Your feet are in the same zenkutsu-dachi position at the finish, but two big lengths forward.

tension in your bent leg. Your Karate movements must be as explosive as a panther's. Animals crouch when getting ready to spring, and in doing so gather the maximum supply of tension. You too must tense at the right moment before speeding forward.

The same principle of catapulting with the aid of a bent supporting leg is also valid for transition into the sideways movements of *kiba-dachi*. Think this over, and attempt catapulting when you practice *kiba-dachi*.

Also practice the giant step backwards. It is like continuous walking, going backwards in the *zenkutsu-dachi*.

Transition forward into zenkutsu-dachi

This is similar to the transition into *kiba-dachi* in that you must change supporting legs. In this instance too, you catapult yourself as you bring up your right foot (Illus. 25) and while you are doing it (Illus. 26), you continue the catapulting force by bringing your left leg up energetically (Illus. 27). You end in the same position of feet but a giant step forward.

Turns in the zenkutsu-dachi stance

In competition, self-defence and in exhibitions (the *kata*), you

Illus. 28

Illus. 29

The 180-degree turn on the spot in zenkutsu-dachi is achieved by a simple ankle pivot.

need to know how to turn in this position. You will use turns mostly in attacking and counter-attacking.

For a 180-degree turn on the spot, feel out with the balls of your feet. Then turn your body around quickly and forcefully, pivoting on the balls of your feet with the weight of your body simultaneously displaced to the new supporting leg (right leg, in Illus. 28 and 29). Stay erect, right hip forward, tense your abdominal wall as you pivot.

Illus. 30   **Illus. 31**
The 180-degree body turn must be made quickly. Move your right foot in a straight line past your supporting leg and ankle, with your knees remaining bent.

For a 180-degree turn with a large step, your center of gravity, as with all movements in Karate, must remain low. In this case, too, feel out with the balls of your feet, then turn your body quickly, moving your right foot (Illus. 30 and 31) in a straight line past your left (rear) foot. Make certain that you execute the turning of your body as a unity. In this way you will perform certain quick turns for the kata.

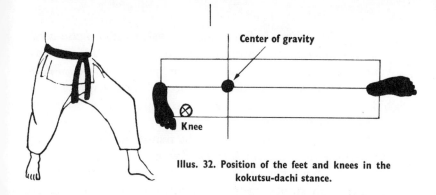

Illus. 32. Position of the feet and knees in the kokutsu-dachi stance.

Kokutsu-dachi, the back stance

Have 70 per cent of the weight of your body on your rear leg, 30 per cent on your front leg (Illus. 32). Your right leg, as in *kiba-dachi* (the straddle-leg stance), is turned slightly to the inside and sharply bent at the knee with tension to the outside. Your heels are in a straight line (Illus. 33). *Kokutsu-dachi* is used almost exclusively in defence.

Illus. 33. In the kokutsu-dachi, the main portion of your weight must be on your rear leg. This is a defensive position.

For practice, move forwards and backwards with *kokutsu-dachi*. It is also important to stay erect, keep your hip forward, and tense your abdominal wall. Turns and steps are possible in *kokutsu-dachi* as in *zenkutsu-dachi*, the forward stance. There is a special possibility here—the 180-degree turn on the spot can be made with your feet remaining on a single line.

Practice all positions, especially the transitions from one to the other—for example, from *kiba-dachi* without moving a step into *kokutsu-dachi* and from that position into *zenkutsu-dachi*, and so on, merely by displacement of weight, turning on the balls of your feet or your heels.

For all movements in all positions, it is always valid to think of the leg behind you, and concentrate on keeping tension there.

Position of the body

Karate is mastery of equilibrium. For that reason, with few exceptions, you do not bend your body backwards. Your spine must always remain straight. You may of course turn your body to the side in order to present as little surface area as possible for your opponent to attack. You turn your body to the side especially for defence, and also to transform the power of simultaneously counter-turning for the counter-attack.

Now that we have looked at the "substructures" which help to make techniques as effective as possible, let's turn to the techniques themselves.

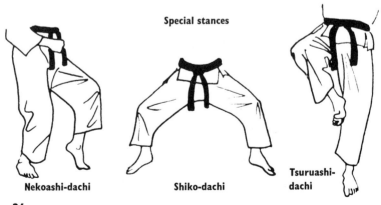

Special stances

Nekoashi-dachi   **Shiko-dachi**   **Tsuruashi-dachi**

Survey of the Techniques

Attack Techniques
    Punching technique (*zuki-waza*)
    Striking technique (*uchi-waza*)
    Kicking technique (*keri-waza*)
    Other (attacks with the head, shoulder, and so on)

Blocking techniques (uke-waza)

You can defend yourself first with your arms and then with your legs. It is advisable to stick to this system and this succession. Frequently, one technique results from the other. If you recognize the common factors, your survey over the whole area of Karate is facilitated. You learn more economically.

Many people imitate advanced learners when they see their free movements. Remember that these advanced learners are able to move with agility because they have studied the basic techniques seriously and learned them correctly. Imitation of advanced students without study and practice yourself can be dangerous for the beginner.

Everyone who wishes to master Karate techniques must practice industriously, and study the basic techniques with understanding and self-criticism. One of the paths is patience.

Other basic stances

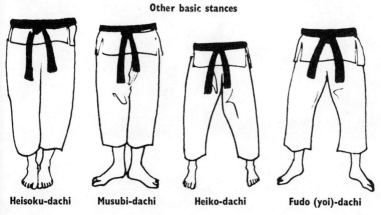

Heisoku-dachi   Musubi-dachi   Heiko-dachi   Fudo (yoi)-dachi

Illus. 35   Illus. 36   Illus. 37

Illus. 38   Illus. 39   Illus. 40

28

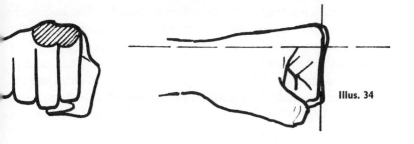

Illus. 34

2. Punching Techniques
(Zuki-waza)

A straight line is the shortest distance between two points. All techniques which steer a straight path to their goal belong to the technique called *seiken-choku-zuki*, the straight thrust with the front of the fist. Illus. 35–37 and 38–40 show how the right fist is cocked, and then thrust forward sharply from the hip. Starting out from the hip with palm up, the fist strikes with palm down, and the wrist tensed.

Position of the fist: Only the knuckles of the index and middle fingers strike the surface (Illus. 34). The fist must extend straight from the wrist so that it does not bend over when it strikes.

Relax your shoulders and sink down. Hold your punching fist palm up so close to your hip that your little finger touches the hip bone and your elbow is pressed to the rear (Illus. 35). Your other hand is extended loosely at a point in front of the center of your body (Illus. 38).

Imagine two lines from your hip bone. One originates at the end of your right pelvic bone and extends to the point in front of your body where your left hand now is. The other originates at your left pelvic bone and extends to the same point.

The punching right fist now advances along the first line, while the left hand recedes smoothly at the same speed back to a fist position along the other line. Just at the instant when the punching right fist is right up front and your left fist is back at your left hip, both fists turn and engage. The right fist turns palm down and the left palm up, ready for the next blow to start. That is the moment to tense your body. To help tensing, exhale at this instant and tense your abdominal wall. Concentrate on your *hara*. The thrust does not come out of your shoulders, but from the middle of your body, from the *hara*. Therefore, be sure you do not let your shoulder go forward.

When you have mastered this fist manoeuvre you will have learned a great part of Karate technique. For that reason, practice it continuously. Just as a master of Judo practices falling before each training session, you practice jabbing with the fist.

Practice this way for each training session, starting from the *hachiji-dachi* (basic stance):

First punch back and forth, slowly and without force, while (a) making sure your elbows brush along your body and that the two straight lines are maintained; then (b) engaging by a synchronized turning of both fists into the final position.

Second, continue to punch slowly, but then tense all your muscles as you turn your fists. All your muscles! For one second. Maintain this tension especially in the side muscles and the abdominal muscles.

Breathing: Breathe in (relaxed), press the air down and punch slowly as you are doing this. Instead of just turning both fists, twist them into final positions, tensing all muscles and exhaling. Then breathe in again, relax, and jab with the other fist.

Now, practice rapid thrusts, 10 with the right hand, then 10 with the left. Do not concentrate on the punching hand, but on the one that is receding. Become conscious of the fact that the receding hand determines the speed of the punching fist. If you concentrate on this, then it will become fact, and will be a great help in increasing speed and bringing your body into tension.

Finally, practice rapid punches alternately with the right and left from *kiba-dachi*, the straddle-leg stance.

Practice the fist punch (*sei-ken*) in this form throughout every training session. As we will see next, the punch with the front of the fist is used in various ways.

Illus. 41   Illus. 42   Illus. 43

As you advance a giant step, you punch with your fist and catapult forwards.
This is the oi-zuki. Advancing leg and fist are on the same side of your body.

The oi-zuki, the lunge punch, same side

With this blow, the punching fist is on the same side of the body as the advancing leg.

Use the catapult-like giant step forward here. The fist strikes at exactly the same moment that the front leg touches down. This technique is highly effective when the high points of tension in your legs and the upper part of your body are simultaneous. Not only the upper part of your body, but your substructure must be stiffly tensed at the moment of striking. This occurs through the *hara*, by stiffening of the abdominal muscles and breathing.

The *oi-zuki* receives its greatest power from the forward movement of your body. For that reason, practice the catapult-like step forward again and again. Let your body shoot forward.

31

Extend your supporting leg energetically. Start your punching fist from your hip at the very moment when your rear leg passes the supporting leg. Your body will therefore fly forward almost as fast as your fist. Make sure the shoulder of your punching arm is not pushed forward. Do not thrust from your shoulder, but from your *hara*. Practice this punch with the giant step or from *hachiji-dachi*. Aim it principally for the solar plexus and the face.

Illus. 44. Beginners practicing the first stage of the gyaku-zuki.

The gyaku-zuki, the reverse punch

In this punch, if the left leg is in front, the punch is made from the right, and vice versa. Therefore the designation, *gyaku*, meaning reversed.

The force for this punch which is more powerful than the *oi-zuki*, comes from a powerful turning of the hip. To be sure, it is not so fast or so direct as the *oi-zuki*. For this reason and others, it is generally used in counter-attacking.

Basically, one can say that the *oi-zuki* (the same-side form) is faster and more direct. With it, you can use every arm technique quickly and directly, so it is good for attack.

While you can use every arm technique in the *gyaku-zuki* (the reverse form), it is preferred for counter-attacking, mainly because of the sharp turning in of the hip.

32

Illus. 45   Illus. 46

In the gyaku-zuki, the punch does not start until the front leg has touched down and you are in the zenkutsu-dachi position.

These two forms are so basic that we must describe them more thoroughly.

The movement of the *gyaku-zuki* is somewhat more difficult than that of the *oi-zuki*. As for time, it takes somewhat longer. In the *gyaku-zuki*, the fist does not strike at the same moment that the front leg touches down—it does not even start until this moment (Illus. 45 and 46). It starts too from a position in which the body is turned 45 degrees away, which you normally take when defending. The advantage of the *gyaku-zuki* is that you employ it without loss of time, and turn a defence into counter-attack. This is valid for all *gyaku* forms.

Analyzing the gyaku-zuki

The *gyaku-zuki* consists of three steps:
1. The position (*zenkutsu-dachi*)
2. The hip turning
3. The fist punch (*zuki*)

In this detailed analysis, we want to consider the fist punch again, and point out what constitutes a good fist punch:

1. The correct path for the punching and receding
2. The speed
3. The concentration of force (tension high point).

Review the forward stance (*zenkutsu-dachi*): The distance between both feet from the side should be 30–39 inches. The hips must be lowered as deeply as possible. (With advanced students, it may perhaps look as if they were holding their hips rather high, but at the moment of striking their legs are tensed and hips lowered.) Tense your abdominal muscles. Your navel must point slightly up.

Hip turning

Now let us practice the agile turning in of the hip, one of the most important and basic movements in Karate. The strong force of the hip must be transmitted to the arm. Without a well controlled hip movement, neither defence nor counter-attack can be effective.

Practicing the hip turning is so important for the beginner, it should be practiced continuously until it is mastered. However, in this respect, even advanced students sin a great deal. Without a good hip turn, your techniques are awkward, your movements stiff, angular, and not very forceful. Practice turning your hips again and again. It is not as simple as it looks at first.

Assume the *zenkutsu-dachi*, the forward starting stance. Rest your hands at your hips. Relax your shoulders and lower them. Tense your abdominal wall slightly. Now turn your body away 45 degrees (Illus. 47). Keep the upper part of your body erect while doing this. Now, by turning your hip back in again, you reach the starting position. At the moment your hip swings back into the starting position, all the muscles of your body must be tensed, especially the muscles of your lower body and the side muscles of your trunk (Illus. 48). The leg behind you must press forward strongly. At this point there is danger that the upper part of your body may incline forwards. To prevent this, always let your navel point slightly upwards.

Illus. 47   **Illus. 48**

Hip turning provides additional power for your gyaku-zuki punching.

Now practice the turning continuously. When you turn away, your body relaxes; when you turn back in, your body tenses. Therefore, breathe in when turning away, breathe out (tensing up) while turning back in. Practice slowly at first, then increasingly faster.

Remember that the turning originates at the hip. Turn only the hip, and your shoulders will follow by themselves. Remain erect, and always have your navel pointing slightly upwards. Press your rear leg forward strongly at the moment of turning back in.

Oi-zuki

Fist punch (zuki)

Read what has already been said about the *seiken-choku-zuki* (page 29).

Concerning the correct path of the fists, remember that your

Illus. 49   **Illus. 50**   **Illus. 51**
In the two-fist punch, you start with palms up, and you reverse this as your fists spring forwards.

hands must move on a straight line that leads from your hip bone out to a point directly in front of the center of your body. Practice this with both fists and with one fist, as shown in Illus. 49, 50 and 51.

At *hachiji-dachi* (the basic position), both fists are at your hips palms up, and your elbows are pressed back (Illus. 49). Now extend both fists at the level of your solar plexus, with your thumbs touching each other slightly, and the palms of your hands pointing down (Illus. 50).

Next, draw your right fist back close to your body and turn it 180 degrees while you are doing this, so it is palm up again. Your elbow must brush the side of your body (Illus. 51). Then let your right fist come forward again. Do this exercise slowly at first, then increasingly faster. Tense your muscles when your returning fist touches your hip. Relax your muscles (inhaling) when the fist goes forward again. First practice with your right fist, then left, then both, etc.

The astonishing jolt of a Karate punch comes from several elements working together at the moment of contact. Every part of your body must be well tuned to every other part in order to make the jab effective. Speed is most important in this. Earlier we said

"Karate is speed transformed into power." The greater the speed, the greater the force.

To give the punching arm more speed, there is a little trick: The receding arm determines the speed. Therefore, draw the receding arm back as quickly and powerfully as possible. At the moment it reaches your hip, tense all your muscles sharply. (Re-read the breathing section of *seiken-choku-zuki*, page 30.) Practice a few times with right, then left.

Concentration of power

The concentrated and simultaneous working together of many muscles is more effective than the working of single muscles at different times, no matter how powerfully they work singly. It is not so simple to tense all your muscles at the proper moment. Therefore, conscious practice is necessary.

Extend both arms so that the fists touch each other slightly (Illus. 52). Now tense all your muscles, especially those of the lower part and sides of your body. Consciously, press your shoulders down towards your chest. Press the air down too and breathe out while doing this (Illus. 53). Then inhale and relax all of your muscles. Practice this.

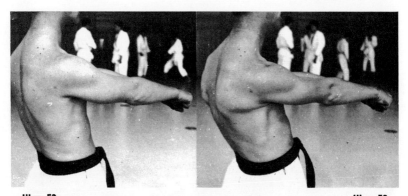

Illus. 52   Illus. 53
Breathing from the hara and pointing your navel slightly upwards give you extra force.

Illus. 54 (left)
Illus. 55 (right)
Practice drawing your
receding arm back rapidly to
a fist at your hip.

Exercise for the receding arm

Take the *zenkutsu-dachi* (the forward stance) turned away by 45 degrees. Your right fist is closed in the originating position on your right hip, your left hand extended to the front (Illus. 54).

Now turn your hip back in sharply and while you are doing

Illus. 56   Illus. 57
Practice stiffening your rear leg as your fist moves forwards in a punch.

this, draw your left hand back rapidly and powerfully on a straight line to a fist. Be sure that your elbows are pressed to your ribcage (Illus. 55). This exercise is to strengthen the sides of your body. The movements of the hip and the receding arm must be synchronized. Practice it, right and left.

Exercise for the rear leg

Take the same starting position. While you are doing this, do not hold your leg stiffly behind you, but relaxed and slightly bent (Illus. 56). Now turn your hip in again sharply, and let your fist start forward. Don't interrupt the movement when your hip reaches its forward position. Meanwhile, extend your rear leg abruptly and tense it as if you were pushing against the floor powerfully with the sole of your foot. By doing this, a counterforce results, which is transmitted through your body to the jabbing fist and increases the force of the punch (Illus. 57).

While you are doing this, check to see that your body remains erect, that you shove your hip forward and that your navel is pointing slightly upwards. Learn and feel consciously in the course of this exercise that the force of *gyaku-suki* (the reverse punch) comes out of the hip *and* out of the rear leg, and that it is transmitted to the punching fist.

The whole gyaku-zuki

Take the left *zenkutsu-dachi* (the forward stance) with your body turned away by 45 degrees. The upper part of your body must be movable, the soles of your feet pressing down on the floor, your knees elastic. Extend your left hand out straight with your elbow relaxed. Put your right fist, palm up, on your right hip, your elbow toward your backbone. Look straight ahead, drawing your chin in slightly.

As your hip is swung back in again, draw your left hand back sharply and make your fist solid while doing this. At the same time, extend your rear leg out powerfully and thrust your right fist forward on a straight line. At the moment your right arm is completely extended and your left fist drawn back to your hip, your entire body must be filled with tension and power. As for breathing, resume the starting position relaxed (breathe in). Exhale at the high tension point.

Pointers to remember

1. Lower your hips as deep as possible and leave the soles of your feet on the floor.

2. Move your arms so that your elbows brush along your body; in this way they will not go to the outside as you are turning your hip.

3. Try consciously not to turn your shoulders, but rather your hips, and let your shoulders follow. The thrust does not come from your shoulder, but from your hip. Relax your shoulders and try to turn your body at the hip.

4. Effective hip turning must be fast.

5. Always be sure that your navel points slightly upwards.

6. Be sure you are breathing correctly while tensing and relaxing.

The two punching techniques *oi-zuki* and *gyaku-zuki* are among the most basic techniques of Karate. For this reason, they must be practiced constantly by both beginners and masters.

Once again, here are the most important characteristics of both techniques:

Oi-zuki. The attack lands as the advancing leg sets down. This is a very fast and direct attack which receives its power from the forward propulsion of the body. For this reason, the forward movement must really be fast.

Gyaku-zuki. A very powerful punch, which gets its power from the sharp turning of the hip. The hip does not start unless the front leg is touched down. *Gyaku-zuki* is mostly used in counter-attacking.

Tate-zuki

Exactly like *seiken-choku-zuki* (the straight punch with the front of your fist), except that your extended fist makes a quarter turn,

Illus. 58

Illus. 59

In tate-zuki (left) the fist makes a quarter turn. In ura-zuki (right) the elbow moves in front of the body.

so that the palm is facing inwards (Illus. 58) instead of a half turn. It is applied in the same-side (*oi-zuki*) and the reverse form (*gyaku-zuki*), above all in close competition.

Ura-zuki

A technique especially used in close fighting. The fist is thrust out, starting from the hip. At the moment of contact it is turned to the outside (palm inwards) and the elbow is shoved somewhat in front of the body (Illus. 59). Tense your stomach and chest muscles above all at the moment of contact.

Mawashi-zuki

Mawashi-zuki

The fist is thrust in a half circle (roundhouse) from the hip, following an outside line unless it makes contact at right angles

The roundhouse punch from the hip (mawashi-zuki) is used most often in counter-attack.

against the temple of the opponent (Illus. 60, 61 and 62). Be sure that your fist really describes a half circle.

This is used mostly in counter-attack in the *gyaku* form in order to utilize the force of the turning in of the hip.

Kagi-zuki

The fist does not move along the body to the front center, but is punched in a hook. The elbow of the punching arm leaves the body sharply at right angles (Illus. 63).

It is used in counter-attack under the defending arm of the opponent (Illus. 64), usually from the *kiba-dachi* (straddle-leg stance).

The two hook type punches (*mawashi-zuki* and *kagi-zuki*) are not easy at first for the beginner to perform to get shock effect. Therefore, practice slowly at first, completely relaxed, and without force. Then tense all your muscles sharply at the moment of contact, especially those muscles at the side of your lower body. Practice breathing exactly as for *seiken-choku-zuki*.

Morote-zuki

Both fists start simultaneously from the hips for the same target (Illus. 65).

In kagi-zuki, swing your elbow out sharply as you strike beneath your opponent's defending arm.

Age-zuki

The starting position is at the hip as for the normal fist punch. The *age-zuki* is actually a blow rather than a punch, for the back of the fist is smashed against the chin of the opponent in an ascending arc by a snapping movement of the elbow (Illus. 66).

Illus. 65   Illus. 66
Morote-zuki (left) is a two-fisted punch. Age-zuki (right) is a punch with an upward swing to catch your opponent under his chin.

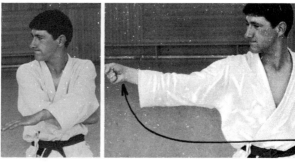

Illus. 67   **Illus. 68**
Riken-uchi is an upward side strike with the back of your fist.

3. Striking Techniques

(Uchi-waza)

In this technique, the striking is usually accomplished by a snapping motion from the elbow. The transmission of force does not occur like a thrust on a straight line, but usually from a half circle. Many striking techniques can also be used in defence.

Illus. 69.
The fist turns at impact in riken-uchi.

Illus. 70. In another type of riken-uchi, the back of the fist strikes downwards from the side.

Riken-uchi (also called ura-ken-uchi)

In the sidewards strike, the back of the fist is used. The fist is propelled from the elbow, crossing the body (left to right in Illus. 67 and 68). At the moment of contact, the fist turns so that the small finger side points down (Illus. 69).

In striking down, the back of the fist is again used in a wide arc with the elbow as the turning point (Illus. 67 and 70), but the fist strikes with palm up.

Riken-uchi is preferred for close fighting, as for an attack on the face or solar plexus. It can be applied to the front also from *zenkutsu-dachi*, the forward stance.

Practice both types of *riken-uchi* in this way:

Starting position: *hachiji-dachi*. Glide from this position into *kiba-dachi* (the straddle-leg) stance and strike with *riken-uchi* while doing this. The back of the fist must strike at the same moment as the leg is put down. Tension peaks in the whole body. Practice to right and left and at right angles to front and rear.

Kentui-uchi (also called tettsui-uchi)

This is exactly the same as *riken-uchi* except that the small finger side of the fist is used in striking a hammer blow.

Tettsui-uchi

Haishu-uchi

In this blow with the back of the hand, the same movement and form of practice are used as with *riken-uchi*. It is especially im-

45

Illus. 71   **Illus. 72**

Haishu-uchi is a strike like riken-uchi but with the back of the open hand.

portant that the back of the hand be turned sharply to the outside at the time of contact (Illus. 71 and 72).

In all Karate techniques in which the open hand and the edge of the hand are used, the thumb is angled down sharply to protect it from injury (Illus. 72).

The *haishu-uchi* technique is used in attacking the diaphragm, face, temples, and ears, and above all in defence.

Open hand (nukite)

Shuto-uchi

The blow with the edge of the hand, *shuto-uchi*, is an effective and well known Karate technique. It also obtains its effect from a snapping motion from the elbow and from turning out of the wrist. There are two different types.

The first type—the blow from the outside to the inside—starts with your thumb. Bend your thumb in sharply and tense your hand (Illus. 73). Be sure that you do not raise the shoulder of your striking arm (Illus. 74). That makes it impossible to tense the side trunk muscles and chest muscles. Strike with the edge of your hand (Illus. 75).

46

Illus. 73   Illus. 74   Illus. 75
Shuto-uchi depends for its effectiveness on a snapping of the elbow as you swing.

Apply this strike in *zenkutsu-dachi* (the forward stance) in the same side and reverse form. In the latter, this edge-of-the-hand technique is especially effective, since the turning in of the hip acts to increase the roundhouse motion of striking.

The second type—the blow from the inside to the outside—starts with bringing the palm of your striking hand to the opposite ear (Illus. 76). Through the snapping motion of the elbow and the turning of the wrist (Illus. 77), this technique gets its effect.

Illus. 76 (left).
Illus. 77 (right).
Striking with the
edge of your
hand is shuto-
uchi.

Illus. 78. Apply shuto-uchi at the level of your opponent's chin, and turn your body away.

At the point of contact, at the level of your opponent's chin, your body may be turned away (Illus. 78). Notice that the surface of your stretching hand faces down obliquely at the moment of contact. Techniques using the edge of the hand are equally effective when executed with the same-side form or the reverse form.

Apply *shuto-uchi* from *zenkutsu-dachi* and from *kiba-dachi*. Later, we will find it in somewhat varied form in defence (see *shuto-uke* and *gedan-uke*).

Empi-uchi backwards (ushiro-empi)

The elbow is an especially powerful and variable weapon in close fighting. Without long boring special training, you can strike with the elbow very effectively. Women can apply the elbow in self-defence especially well.

The backward blow with the elbow (*ushiro-empi*) you have already practiced many a time completely unconsciously: it is nothing more than the movement of the receding arm in the fist technique. (Pointer for trainers: the *ushiro-empi* results as a sort of by-product from the learning of the fist punch.)

In Illus. 79, your opponent has wrapped his arms around you and grabbed your upper arm from the rear. How do you get loose? You bring both your hands together in front of your chest, with the palms of your hands up. Now assume the *kiba-dachi* (straddle-leg) position to the left, and thrust your arms forward at the same

Illus. 79   Illus. 80   Illus. 81
Escape from a bear hug ending in ushiro-empi, a backwards blow with your elbow.

time. While doing this, rotate your elbows and turn your hands (still together) so that at the end your palms are facing down. In doing this, a lever effect occurs in your upper arms which breaks your opponent's embrace. By lowering your hip to the side at the same time, you will break free (Illus. 80). In the course of this entire movement, your spine must remain vertical. Start the movement from your hip (from the *hara*). Once free, you need only to rip your extended right arm down and to the rear. The *empi-uchi* (backward blow with the elbow) hits exactly in the pit of your opponent's stomach (Illus. 81).

Empi-uchi to the front (mae-empi)

Start with your left fist at your hip. Your right hand swings out to the front, relaxed (Illus. 82). Now the elbow of your right arm is thrust straight to the front towards its target as your arm tenses and your wrist turns over (Illus. 83). The targets are usually the solar plexus or the ribs. However, this blow can also be aimed against the head (Illus. 84). (See next page.)

Your body may be turned in the course of this, but remember that you should be anchored so that your navel always points up slightly. Otherwise, your shoulder can very easily come forward in this technique.

Illus. 82

Illus. 83

Illus. 84

Empi-uchi is an effective elbow strike. To the front (called mae-empi) it can be aimed at the solar plexus or ribs or at the head. See page 49.

Yoko-empi is an elbow thrust to the side.

Practice this with the same side and reverse forms, out of *zenkutsu-dachi*, the forward stance.

Empi-uchi to the side (yoko-empi)

Thrust your elbow sharply to the side and turn your wrist in doing this (Illus. 85- 86). The elbow of your striking arm will hit exactly on the nipple of the opponent's chest (Illus. 86). If it were to continue, your elbow would describe a slight arc to the rear, but you would no longer be able to tense the muscles of your lower body and the muscles at the side of your torso.

The *yoko-empi* is used almost exclusively from the *kiba-dachi* (straddle-leg) position. Practice it starting from *hachiji-dachi*, the basic position. Glide to the right, to the left, at right angles, right and left forwards and backwards, into *kiba-dachi*. While doing this, complete the *yoko-empi* simultaneously each time you place your leg down. This is the same practice form as in *riken-uchi* (the sidewards strike) out of *kiba-dachi*. Always strike with your elbow, which points the direction.

Empi-uchi upwards (age-empi)

Start in position with your fist at your hip. Now swing your elbow sharply upwards (Illus. 87) and turn your fist while you are doing this, so that your palm faces your ear. The point of

51

Illus. 88

Illus. 87. Age-empi is an
upward blow with the elbow.

Illus. 89

your elbow will strike the opponent in front of the middle of his
chin (Illus. 89). For that reason, your body must be turned away
somewhat, your head inclined away.

The *age-empi* can also be struck to the front against your
opponent's solar plexus (Illus. 88).

Application of *age-empi* is mostly out of *zenkutsu-dachi* (the
forward position) in the reverse form (as counter-attack) or the
same-side form.

Shita-empi

Illus. 90   Illus. 91

Illus. 92   Illus. 93

Empi-uchi down (shita-empi)

Illus. 90–93 show downward striking with the elbow against your opponent's chest and neck. The elbow techniques all require short, sharp action and immediate release (tension and relaxation).

Practice all elbow techniques this way: Starting position normal in *hachiji-dachi*, the basic position.

Tempo 1: *mae-empi* (to the front), sharp tensing up, immediate release, and then

Tempo 2: *yoko-empi* (to the side), then

Tempo 3: *ushiro-empi* (backwards), then

Tempo 4: *age-empi* (upwards), and

Tempo 5: *empi-uchi* down (*shita-empi*).

After short relaxation (inhaling), count again: 1, 2, 3, 4, 5, perform the actions, and go on. Finally, carry out all techniques at the same tempo. After this, practice to the left.

Here is a practice form of the fist blow in connection with *ushiro-empi*: Rip the extended arm back to *ushiro-empi* (tempo 1), then thrust your fist of the same arm forwards (tempo 2), then do both techniques at one speed. Give a short, sharp exhale at the moment of the fist blow to the front.

Once again for review:

Do you still remember that as each technique is carried out, your navel must point slightly upwards? Do you always breathe correctly in a way that helps you tense and relax alternately? In executing each technique, and each movement, do you still recall that every fast, powerful movement must originate from the hip, that the *hara* is your focus, which you must preserve, so that you do not lose your balance? Always imagine that your "middle" is just below your navel. Practice correct breathing to help you strengthen this *hara*. Only then will each one of your movements and techniques be sure and powerful, starting from your inner balance, your *hara*, surely and powerfully.

Be increasingly conscious of the fact that the strength for your fist jab, for example, does not come from the arm—as the beginner thinks—but from the *hara*. Correct breathing helps you a great deal in doing this—a portion of the air is pressed down against the abdominal wall as you exhale.

Illus. 94. Quick kick is the rule in Karate.

4. Kicking Techniques
(Keri-waza)

The use of the leg as a weapon is a unique characteristic of Karate. In daily life, your legs are not utilized in varied activities or in as many different ways as your arms. For that reason, your legs must be exercised persistently, for you to use them well as weapons. When using kicking techniques, you must pay particular attention to the supporting leg. In order to preserve your balance,

Illus. 95
Start

Illus. 96
Mae-geri-ke-age

Illus. 97
Mae-geri-ke-komi

your supporting leg must stand strongly, particularly in the direction of the thrust of your foot. In addition, it must be able to absorb the shock when your foot strikes its target. For this reason, the supporting leg must always be slightly bent and elastic at the knee. During the thrust, the entire sole of your foot must remain on the ground.

The instantaneous pulling back of your thrusting leg, which must take place as quickly as the actual thrust itself, is very important for maintaining your balance. Not only do your leg muscles work when using leg techniques, but, as is the case with every Karate technique, you must use your entire body as well, and, in this case, the power of your hip particularly.

Mae-geri, the front kick

In *mae-geri*, the ball of the foot strikes. Therefore, your toes must be sharply clenched in at an angle. There are two types of *mae-geri*:

1. *Mae-geri-ke-age*

In this kick, it is chiefly the snapping motion of the knee that is utilized. The ball of your foot thrusts upwards ("age" means "lift") and strikes your partner's chin, armpit, chest, or stomach, like an uppercut from below. Starting from the *hachiji-dachi* (basic) position, draw up your knee as high as possible towards your chest. In doing this, keep your foot parallel to the floor, your toes angled sharply away (Illus. 95). Without interruption, now propel your foot up (Illus. 96) and spring back into the starting position with the foot at the supporting knee (Illus. 95) in a single uninterrupted movement. Note that the supporting knee and leg remain stationary. Use tempo 1 for the ripping up of the knee, the kick, and the springing back of the foot to the knee. Use tempo 2 for placing down your foot—this is a separate tempo speed.

Be sure that the toes of your supporting leg point straight ahead and that the knee and the toes of your kicking leg point straight ahead as well. Only in this way can you concentrate all of the muscles of your body into the thrust.

2. *Mae-geri-ke-komi*

In this technique, the foot is thrust straight to the target, noticeably using the hip (Illus. 97). When doing this, you can strike with the ball of your foot or your heel. Strike with your heel when practicing, angle up your toes sharply when doing it.

The *mae-geri* is usually carried out from the *zenkutsu-dachi* or forward position with one leg behind. Use the *mae-geri-ke-age* when your distance from your partner is not too great and when he is bent slightly forward. Use the *mae-geri-ke-komi* from a greater distance—it is very powerful as the hip is thrust in the direction of the target.

Mae-geri

Illus. 98   **Practice**   Illus. 99

Illus. 100. Ke-age   **Illus. 101. Ke-komi**

Follow Illus. 98–101 for practice forms of *mae-geri-ke-age* and *ke-komi*. Your partner stretches out his hand at the level of his chin. You stand in front of him in such a way that his fingertips touch your chin (Illus. 98). Now assume *zenkutsu-dachi* from the rear (Illus. 99). First kick *mae-geri-ke-age* with the ball of your foot to the palm of your partner (Illus. 100). Place your leg down

58

again to *zenkutsu-dachi* (Illus. 99), then execute *mae-geri-ke-komi* towards his solar plexus (Illus. 101). Thrust your hip strongly in the direction of the target. With the *ke-komi*, you are a good arm's length further away from the target than with *ke-age*.

Practice stance for mae-geri exercises.

For further practice, stand in another basic position, *heisoku-dachi*, knees and feet together, large toes touching each other, knees slightly bent (Illus. 102 and 103).

Now do *mae-geri-ke-age* 10 times to the right, then 10 to the left, and while doing it, try to kick as high as possible. (Between each blow, set your leg down.) You will notice that even when doing *ke-age*, your hip must be shoved slightly forward. Above all, you will find that your knee must be taken as high up towards the chest as possible, and that after the kick it must return to this position. This exercise is also very good for your balance. Lifting your knee up high is very important in all leg techniques. For that reason, you need a few more exercises which force you to get your knee up as high as possible.

Knee exercises

Draw your knee up as high as possible to your chest and hold it with your hands. Remain erect while doing this and do not bend away at the hip (Illus. 104). Alternate left and right legs.

Practicing the mae-geri over an obstacle

For best results, stand behind an obstacle, such as a low bench,

Illus. 105

a tight string, belt, or similar, in the *zenkutsu-dachi* or *heisoku-dachi* position, and kick out so closely that your foot in *mae-geri* just passes over the obstacle without touching it. Your knee has to be drawn up (Illus. 105 and 106).

Now practice *mae-geri* on signal. The knee, to go past the obstacle, must be up very high towards your chest before and after the kick.

Target practice

Your partner again stands in front of you and stretches out his hand at chin level. You kick for it 10 times from *zenkutsu-dachi* with *mae-geri-ke-age*, using your right leg, then 10 times with your left leg. Now your partner holds his hand next to him at the level of his stomach so that his palm is towards you. Kick with the ball of your foot and, when kicking, throw your hip in the direction of the kick.

A little variant for advanced students: Your partner changes the position of his hand after every kick so that you have to adjust quickly to a new target.

Illus. 106

Yoko-geri, the side kick

In doing this, kick with the outside edge of your foot. Your foot must be positioned obliquely in such a way that the sole of your foot is as parallel as possible with the floor (Illus. 109). There are two types of *yoko-geri*:

1. *Yoko-geri-ke-age*

You must raise your knee as high as possible (Illus. 107) and sling your foot out from the knee without interruption (Illus. 108). Spring back to the knee position (Illus. 107) and place it down.

2. *Yoko-geri-ke-komi*

In this case, you start from the same position (Illus. 107), but

Yoko-geri

Illus. 110

at the moment of striking, your hip is thrust in the direction of the goal (Illus. 109 and 110), and your foot is turned sole down as much as possible. Do not lean the upper part of your body too much in the opposite direction from the target, but push your arms in the direction of the target. In Illus. 110 you see the direct use of the hip clearly.

Illus. 111. You can practice Karate kicks out-of-doors as well as indoors.

Practice these kicks from all positions, especially from *kiba-dachi* (the straddle-leg position) in transition and in turning, but also especially out of *zenkutsu-dachi* (the forward position) with your rear leg.

Illus. 112. Gymnastic exercise to strengthen knee and leg.

Functional gymnastic exercises

Lift your knee as high as possible with the aid of your hand (Illus. 112), alternately left and right.

Practice with a partner: Stand in front of your partner in *kiba-dachi* so that you turn your side to him. Measure off the distance so that with one transition step you come into attacking distance. Now take a transition step towards your partner, who is standing in *hachiji-dachi* (the basic position), draw your leg as high up as possible, and move as if to clobber him in the chest with *yoko-geri-ke-komi*. Never use full strength, but just touch your partner. Now your partner takes your foot in both his hands and draws it higher. Make sure your supporting leg is in the correct position. Move your arms and the upper part of your body towards your partner and stay as erect as possible. When your partner releases your foot, place it down towards him in *kiba-dachi* and follow with a transition step back into the starting position. Practice

10 times to the right, then partners change and repeat, then 10 times to the left, then change and repeat.

Kicking above an obstacle

This is similar to *mae-geri* (the front kick), but don't use a bench, rather a rope or two belts tied together and held by two partners 32 inches from the floor. Take your position at the side of it in *kiba-dachi*, take your transition step, then draw your knee up high, and kick above the obstacle, put your leg back, and place it down in *kiba-dachi* facing the rope. Then back to the starting position with a transition step. If you fail to lift your knee high up to your chest before and after, you will get stuck on the obstacle.

Heisoku-dachi

Yoko-geri from heisoku-dachi

Lift your knee up rapidly, and propel your foot to the side and upwards without interrupting the movement. Note the participation of your hip, as in the case of *ke-age*. Bring your foot back to your knee and then place it down again into *heisoku-dachi* (knees and feet close together). This is a very good balance exercise. Turn the upper part of your body in the direction of the target. Try 10 kicks right, then 10 left. Be sure that when you set down your foot, your knees and your big toes are next to each other.

Finally, a somewhat more difficult exercise:

Draw your right leg up high to the side and hold it with your right hand, as in the exercise for *yoko-geri*. Now kick it sideways with *yoko-geri* (*ke-age* or *ke-komi*) and then let it spring back into your hand. Without placing your right leg down, kick 10 times, then do the same with your left leg. One purpose is to hold your balance so well that your supporting leg remains in the same spot throughout the powerful kicks. Do not bend your hip. Remain erect with the upper part of your body, and look in the direction of your target.

Illus. 113

Illus. 114

Practice kicking ke-komi and
ke-age with a partner.

Illus. 115

Practice with a partner

Take your partner by the sleeve. Lift your knee (Illus. 113) and
kick first with *ke-komi* towards his upper thigh (Illus. 114), then
draw your leg back and put it down. Then kick with *ke-age*
towards his armpit (Illus. 115). You first lift up your knee quickly
and then propel your foot towards the target without interruption.
Now it's your partner's turn to kick. Keep changing sides.

Target practice

Practice kicking towards the hand of your partner as in *mae-
geri*. In addition to practice of the *ke-age* alone, there is another
exercise: Tie a belt at the level of your chest around a projection.
Hold the end in one hand and then strike the belt with a *ke-age*
kick from below. Pay attention to correct position of your feet.

Illus. 116   Illus. 117

Ushiro-geri, kick to the rear

In this kick, you strike with your heel. You again draw up your knee, and then thrust your foot directly to the rear (Illus. 116 and 117). Upper thighs should keep contact with each other as long as possible, and your leg must be extended as completely as possible (Illus. 118).

Illus. 118.
Ushiro-geri.

Ushiro-geri, the backwards kick.

Rapid withdrawal of your leg is also especially important in this kick in order not to lose your balance. Bend the upper part of your body, but not too far away, and rather attempt to launch it in the direction of your target.

Stretching exercises for ushiro-geri

Stand in the *heisoku-dachi* position (knees and feet together) in front of your partner again and turn your back to him. Then take bearings over your shoulder and strike at his solar plexus with *ushiro-geri* (not too forcefully). When you do this, you should just touch his chest (Illus. 119). Your partner then grabs your foot with both hands and lifts it up. Pay attention to the correct position of your foot (heel up) and to your supporting leg. The upper part of your body should be in the direction of the target.

Another form of exercise: First kick forward with *mae-geri* and then, quickly and powerfully, without placing your foot down, kick to the rear with *ushiro-geri* (Illus. 120). Then you can also add a *yoko-geri* as well, without placing your foot down. Balance! Do this exercise several times in succession without touching down the leg that is doing the striking. But make each single kick of your foot powerful and exact.

68

Three steps in performing mawashi-geri.

Mawashi-geri, the roundhouse kick

In doing this kick, you utilize the snapping movement of your knee and the turning movement of your hip in order to attack your opponent from the side with the ball or rear of your foot.

Lift up your leg, keeping it horizontal to the floor (Illus. 121) and then propel it rapidly forwards without interruption (Illus. 122). While you are doing this, turn your body along with the motion so that your supporting leg is turned 45 degrees to the side

Mawashi-geri

(90 degrees at the most). Strike sharply and snap your knee back quickly, then assume the starting position again with your supporting leg turning back in (Illus. 123). Try in this case to hold the upper part of your body as straight as possible.

Exercises for mawashi-geri

Starting from the *hachiji-dachi* (basic) position, lift up your right leg horizontally and to the side (Illus. 124), using both hands (right hand on your ankle, left hand on your knee). Do this alternately with your right leg and then your left. When you do this, your knee must point slightly upwards. Keep the inner edges of your other foot on the floor.

One more exercise on the floor: Sit with both your legs stretched out in front of you. Then bend back your right leg so that the entire inner surface of the leg touches the floor. (This is the same position the leg will take—but in the air—in *mawashi-geri*.) Then rock forward twice with outstretched arms so that your forehead touches your knee. Then turn the upper part of your body to the rear with outstretched arms, and rock twice to the rear, twice to the front again, and so on.

Stretching exercise with a partner: Stand in the left *zenkutsu* (forward) position, your partner too. Then thrust with *mawashi-geri* so that your foot strikes past his neck. (Do not put any force into the kick.) Your partner catches your leg (Illus. 125) and straightens it up more and more. It is all right if it "pulls." Pay attention to the correct position of your supporting leg (do not turn it too far to the side). Extend your attacking leg and hold the upper part of your body straight. Let it loose—put it down. Now it's your partner's turn. Following this, practice the exercise to the left as well.

Now a somewhat more difficult exercise: Starting from the position of the first exercise (drawing up your leg with your hands) strike with a *mawashi-geri*, let your knee spring back, catch it with your hands and kick again without putting it down. Do this 10 times. When this exercise is working well and your supporting leg remains on the same spot while you are kicking, you have achieved good balance. In addition, practice this from the *heisoku-dachi*

Illus. 124

Illus. 125

Exercises for mawashi-geri.

position (knees and feet together), kick at a right angle to the direction of your foot, and turn back again to the *heisoku-dachi* position.

Some more types of exercise: Advance in the *zenkutsu-dachi* (forward) position with *mawashi-geri*. Advance in the *kokutsu-dachi* (back stance) position with *mawashi-geri*.

A form of exercise with a partner: Stand in the *zenkutsu-dachi* position to the left. Your partner should stand opposite you in the *zenkutsu-dachi* position to the right; his shoulders should be turned away at a 45-degree angle. Now you can strike your partner's chest at exactly a right angle from the side using *mawashi-geri* from the right. Now your partner should take one step backwards as you put down the leg with which you were kicking. You can now kick his chest again immediately, using *mawashi-geri* from the left. Advance continuously with *mawashi-geri* from the right and from the left. When you reach the end of the available space, return to where you started. Now let your partner take his turn. When you are doing this exercise always have a target in mind. That develops the feeling for distance which you absolutely have to have when practicing Karate. In addition, you have to adapt yourself to your partner's movements, something which must also be developed in actual Karate.

Kansetsu-geri

Fumi-komi, the stamping kick (also called kansetsu-geri)

This is a downward-directed kick which you can use forwards, sidewards, or to the rear against the shin, the bridge of the foot, or the back of the knee. It can also be used against an opponent who is on the ground. You strike with your heel or with the outside edge of your foot. This blow is not basically different from the other foot techniques except that it must be "stamped" downwards in a *ke-komi* manner.

Hiza-geri, the kick with the knee

Like the elbow, the knee is a very powerful weapon in close fighting. The knee technique can be a by-product in the course of *mae-geri*. It is nothing more than lifting your knee sharply

Illus. 126. Hiza-geri, the knee kick used in close fighting.

against your partner's chest before you actually perform the kick with your foot. (Illus. 126). Use it in self-defence in the course of being grasped by your opponent's hands, or being choked, or when you are being grabbed at the shoulders, etc.

In concluding, we must examine two more kicking techniques called Tobi in Japanese, which have a sensational effect—this is the reason you frequently see them in photos. These are attacks with your foot from the air and from jumping.

Illus. 127. The advancing foot attack from the air— called mae-tobi-geri.

Mae-tobi-geri or ni-dan-geri

In this advancing foot attack from the air, you can kick once, twice, or three times (Illus. 127). If you find you are merely kicking the air with your foot attack, then step to your left, for example, and kick to the right. This is not an especially difficult kick to learn. However, to deceive your opponent with your first attack, start by kicking towards his chest, or strike his cover (defence) out of the way and follow this up with a second attack. Then it becomes more significant.

Practice in this way: If you are kicking with your right leg, advance a step to the right and then *mae-geri* to the left without interruption. Immediately after doing this, spring sideways to the right and do *mae-geri* into the air. Practice for a while in this

73

Illus. 128. Yoko-tobi-geri is generally considered a beautiful attack.

manner. Then increase the power you put into your jump to the side. Take a short run, jump to the side, then first kick into the air to the left, and finally make your actual attack against the opponent's face to your right. You will notice that you will no longer have difficulty in kicking twice with your foot in the air after this preliminary exercise.

If possible, practice this attack with a tall sandbag. Spring up from a low position with at most a run of one step. Also try to jump up from a very deep position with the aid of the tension in your legs without a running start. (If the leg with which you are kicking is your right leg, then your right leg is in front.)

Yoko-tobi-geri

This is a very beautiful attack. It starts from a jump and there are a few difficulties learning how to perform it. Nevertheless, a good Karateka should take the trouble to learn it.

74

The *yoko-tobi-geri*, actually an attack to the side with your foot in the air, requires you to jump past your opponent and then kick to the side. The greatest difficulty is that the leg from which you jump must be slapped up against the attacking leg as you finish the attack with your foot (Illus. 128).

Now start the exercise as follows: With the left leg the jumping leg, first jump up and down several times in one spot with both legs. Continue, but after every second hop, slap the foot of your supporting leg (the right) to the knee of your jumping leg (the left). Every other time, make a hop without slapping your springing leg. Hop this way for some time. Doing this, slapping the foot of your supporting leg to your jumping leg, will become so automatic that in a short time you will be doing it like a reflex.

As the next step, take a running start, spring up quickly, and kick to the side with your attacking leg. (You do not need to jump high at all.) Probably you will discover for yourself the next difficulty: Your arms will be floating around in the air. You will succeed that much better in bringing your arms down, the more intensively you have practiced the preliminary exercise of slapping the foot of your supporting leg on your springing leg. You can concentrate on your arms much more easily if you no longer have to pay conscious attention to your legs.

The next step then is to practice the actual *yoko-tobi-geri* with a sandbag. Illus. 129 shows *yoko-tobi-geri* in a match.

Illus. 129. Yoko-tobi-geri in a match.

Exercises for foot techniques

Here is an exercise you can do at home (you need only a few minutes) or as a setting-up exercise preceding a practice session. It is useful for all foot techniques because it especially develops the power for the snapping movement of your knee.

1. As a daily exercise, lift your right thigh parallel to the ground from the *hachiji-dachi* (basic) position. Let your foot snap forwards quickly 10 times. Do the same exercise with your left leg. Then lift your right thigh up to the side and snap your foot to the side 10 times. Then the left leg. Pay attention to the correct position of your feet. You will notice the increase in power in your foot techniques very quickly, and you will also find this exercise naturally good training for balance.

The feet are very powerful weapons with a wide range. However, in order to be able to use them effectively, you must practice leg techniques continuously in many forms.

2. An indispensable aid for developing exactness is target practice. You must be able to strike right in the bull's-eye with your feet. Here are a few more ideas for target practice to train your eye: Suspend a small ball (for example, a tennis ball on a string) at chest level. Kick at it with all your strength so that your kick stops in front of it or only touches it lightly. First kick 10 times to the right with *mae-geri-ke-age*, and then to the left. After doing this, practice the same thing with *yoko-geri-ke-age* and then with *mawashi-geri*. Then, after some time, hang the ball up somewhat higher—at a maximum, at chin height. Be sure when doing the *mae-geri* that you touch the ball lightly with the BALL of your foot. You will develop a very good eye after some time with this exercise. You can also use a partner as a target. He should take the *kiba-dachi* (straddle-leg position) in front of you. Aim for his chin in the same manner.

3. A very advantageous exercise for foot techniques is a combination of kicks. Here is an excellent combination which you should practice in every training session: Advance with *mae-geri* (front kick) to the right and to the left, then with *yoko-geri* (side kick) to the right and to the left, then with *ushiro-geri* (kick to the rear) to the right starting from the turning of your body, and then

Kansetsu-geri   **Ushiro-geri**

mae-geri once again to the left. Thus, you will advance continuously in the same direction always alternating your right and left legs. Pay attention first to drawing your knee up high in every technique. As you advance with the foot techniques, throw your body (the *hara*) forwards.

4. Your partner stands before you. Your task is to drive him off by advancing so quickly and taking up so much space that your partner can hardly keep up with you as he goes backwards. This exercise has the additional advantage for you of always keeping a target for your foot techniques before your eyes so that you do not merely have to kick into empty air. Covering a great deal of ground while advancing with foot techniques is naturally an especially great advantage in a fight.

Further combinations which you can practice: Advance with *yoko-geri* to the left and then do *mawashi-geri* (roundhouse kick) to the right without a pause. In this case, you can throw your body into the second technique very nicely. *Mae-geri* and *yoko-geri* is a further combination, or the reverse, *yoko-geri* and *mae-geri*.

The most important thing for all leg techniques is lifting your knee swiftly and powerfully. The decisive thing here is whether you come up high enough with your knee technique and whether your kick is swift and powerful. Practice all techniques starting from the *heisoku-dachi* position (knees and feet together), first snapping up your knee while you are doing this, and then letting your foot snap out high without interruption.

5. There is another nice exercise which develops strength for pulling up your knee: Lean against a wall with your arms extended. Your body should be at approximately a 45-degree angle to the wall. Now lift your knees alternately to your chest.

Something more about the use of the kicks: Kicking with your feet is most effective at stomach level and lower. High kicks can be warded off more easily and put you in danger. For that reason, use high kicks only when you can execute them quickly, precisely and right in the bull's-eye.

"Stopping short" as you did with the arm technique is also valid for the leg technique. Foot techniques must also be stopped with millimeter accuracy. What helps you here is the tension in your lower body (*hara*), which makes the technique highly effective.

In order to give your foot technique the power that originates from the *hara*, your hip must not be bent in at the moment of stopping, and the upper part of your body should not be bent away. These bends prevent you from being able to tense your lower stomach. Keep in mind that if a foot technique is to be effective, your attacking foot must be invisible from your opponent from the moment it leaves the ground. Your foot must be rushed to its target with a whipping motion and then sprung back again.

5. Defence Techniques
(Uke-waza)

This chapter should actually precede the chapter on techniques for attacking. The fact of the matter is that the most important thing in true Karate is defence. This also means that the use of Karate for purposes of attack is not part of the real essence of Karate. However, the presentation of defence has been delayed on purpose, for you can understand the defences better if you know what types of attacks there are.

In Karate, the techniques of defence have a shock effect like the attacks. For this reason, by using a good defence you can rob your opponent of any further desire to attack.

First, here are some basic considerations about defence technique: By defence, we mean every activity which is suited to making an opponent's attack ineffective. The entire activity of defence must result in the opponent desisting from further attacks, or becoming incapable of any further attack because of an immediate counter-attack. Now, if you consider the problem you will find that there are four types of defences:

1. Good defensive techniques cause such great pain that the opponent loses his eagerness to continue attacking.

2. Good defensive techniques lead to a subsequent counter-attack.

3. Without defending yourself directly, you avoid the opponent's attack by turning your body swiftly and make a Karate attack yourself at the same time.

4. You make a Karate attack before your opponent attacks—in other words, you beat your opponent to the draw.

In this chapter, only the purely defensive techniques will be covered. Complete defensive actions will wait until later.

Basic principles

Every defence receives its decisive force by turning away your hips and, by doing this, the upper part of your body. Be conscious of turning with your hip and see that the upper part of your body is carried along. (See also the remarks about *gyaku-zuki*—page 34 —in the section on "turning the hip.") It is not your shoulders which turn, but your hip—sharply and forcefully—carrying along the upper part of your body. Turning your body away in the course of defence has two decisive advantages: In doing this you offer your opponent very little surface to attack. Since your body is turned approximately 45 degrees to the side, you are already standing in a position ready to counter-attack in the *gyaku* form. For this reason, your counter-attack can take place swiftly and forcefully without losing any time.

The basic principle in defence for the beginner is that it be undertaken from the same side: For example, if your left leg is forward, then you must defend to the left, etc. It is only in these circumstances that the two advantages mentioned become valid.

You learned in the case of *oi-zuki* (the lunge punch) that the technique performed from the same side is the more direct and more rapid. Now, when you are defending yourself, you must be equally direct and quick. Your defence must be triggered off at the same moment as you put down your leg. Immediately thereafter you can turn in your hip sharply, and from the turned-away position of your body, begin the counter-attack. (The advanced student must also be able to defend in the *gyaku* form.)

Keep in mind that this powerful turning back and forth of your hip must be clearly visible. Later on are exercises especially tailored for this turning of your hip. However, pay attention to it consciously even now.

Since attacks are possible on the face and neck, on the upper part of the body above the belt, and on parts of the body below the belt, we correspondingly distinguish three levels of attack:

> *jodan*—higher level
> *chudan*—middle level
> *gedan*—lower level

There are specific defences against attacks on each of the levels. We will begin with a defence directed at attacks on the lower level, attacks with the feet.

Lower Level Defence (gedan)

Illus. 130   **Illus. 131**

In gedan-barai, a backwards step and a sharp lowering of an arm act as a basic defence on the lower level.

Gedan-barai or gedan-uke

The attacking limbs are struck aside by a sharp downward blow of your lower arm. As far as the motion is concerned, the *gedan-barai* is exactly like the *shuto-uchi* from the inside to the outside (reread the description on page 47), except that the movement of the arm giving the blow is downwards and that the hand is closed to a fist.

In principle, the defences of *gedan-barai* can be applied out of any position. However, practice every time in the *zenkutsu-dachi* (forward) position. Starting from the position of *hachiji-dachi* with your right arm up high (Illus. 130), step back with your left foot, reach out and strike downwards simultaneously (Illus. 131). When doing this, your wrist will turn to the outside. The defence comes to a stop at the moment your rear leg is placed downward. In the course of this, turn your hip away sharply. The fist of your defending arm will be in a position approximately 10 inches above your knee (Illus. 131). The defending is done with the external edge of your lower arm approximately two inches above your wrist.

Gedan-shuto-uke, see *shuto-uke* (page 85).

Illus. 132   **Illus. 133**

Juji-uke is a defence used mainly against front kicks. Crossed fists interposed cause the attack to be blocked.

Juji-uke or downward X-block

This defence is used particularly against kicks. To be sure, the kick must be caught in its first stage. For this reason, the defence is usually used against a kick to the front in *zenkutsu-dachi* position. When doing this, hold the upper part of your body straight. Your fists start from your right hip (or from both hips). If you are right-handed, your right fist will be above your left one (Illus. 132). Step forward in the *zenkutsu-dachi* position with your right or left foot (Illus. 133). Your fists remain vertical.

Middle Level Defence (chudan)

Illus. 134   Illus. 135

In soto-uke defence, you start your fist behind your ear, and propel it forwards
until it is in front of your opponent's chest.

Soto-uke (use of outer edge of forearm)

This is a defence using the outer (*soto*) edge of the lower arm.
As far as the movements are concerned, this technique is the same
as *shuto-uchi* (see page 46), except that your hand is closed in a
fist. Your fist starts behind your right ear (Illus. 134) and comes
to a stop in front of your opponent's chest. Turn your wrist completely so that the back of your hand faces downward. Turn your
body from the hip (Illus. 135). The elbow of the arm used for
hitting should be above the middle of the thigh of the leg which
you have forward. This is used principally from the *zenkutsu-dachi*
and the *kiba-dachi* (forward and straddle-leg) positions.

Illus. 136 shows a defence with *soto-ude-uke*. In this case, the
fist is turned downwards, but the outer edge of the arm is used.
(See next page.)

Illus. 136. Soto-ude-uke is a defence in which the outer edge of your forearm is used.

Illus. 137   Illus. 138

The uchi-uke defence is difficult to learn.

Uchi-uke

This is the defence with the inner (*uchi*) edge of the lower arm. Your fist swings from below upwards with your elbow as a turning point. It comes to a stop opposite the shoulder on the same side. When you start, the palm of your hand faces down at the left hip (Illus. 137). In the final position, the palm of your hand faces up (Illus. 138). Pay attention to this, as you need to have your elbow in position in front of your body and not to the side. It is somewhat difficult for the beginner to introduce a shock effect into this technique. Later in the book, suitable exercises will be given for all the defence techniques.

Illus. 139   **Illus. 140**

One shuto-uke defence with the edge of the hand.

Shuto-uke

This is the defence with the edge of your hand. It is very fast and can be used in many situations, but is used principally from the *kokutsu-dachi* (back stance) position.

As far as the movements are concerned, this is just like *shuto-uchi* from the inside to the outside (reread the section on page 47) and also like *gedan-uke* (the lower level defence).

85

Illus. 141   Illus. 142

In shuto-uke, one hand remains in front of your chest.

Differences: (1) The angle of the arm doing the hitting (Illus. 139 and 141), and (2) the returning hand remains like a plate before your chest (Illus. 140 and 142).

At the beginning, it is very difficult to get shock effect into the arm doing the hitting, while still stopping the arm at the correct angle. Be sure the edge of your hand is straight with your wrist (Illus. 140 and 142), and is the straight continuation of your lower arm.

Shuto-uke can also be used as a defence against attacks on your face (*jodan-shuto-uke*). In this case, you defend as in *age-uke* (see page 91), except that the edge of your open hand strikes the attacking arm in an upward direction.

There is also a defence using the edge of your hand in a downward blow (*gedan-shuto-uke*). It is exactly like *gedan-barai*, only using an open hand.

Shuto-uke defence at the chudan (middle) level.

Always plan to strike with the edge of your hand in a straight line at the attacking limbs rather than in an arc. Or expressed differently: strike the attacking arm with the edge of your hand in a straight oblique line. Do not turn your wrists until the last moment, but turn your body sharply to the side while striking. Now, if you watch your tension and your breathing at the moment of striking, your defence will soon have the necessary shock effect.

Exercises with a partner

You both stand in the *hachiji-dachi* (basic) position, and your partner extends his fist to your solar plexus. Stand so close that his fist touches your chest (Illus. 143). Now glide away towards the inside at an angle of 45 degrees. While doing this, defend yourself with your left arm (Illus. 144). Hit his arm obliquely with the

Illus. 143   Exercise   Illus. 144

Illus. 145. An exercise to perfect your edge-of-the-hand defences.

edge of your hand. The tips of your fingers must be directly above the tip of your forward foot.

Now assume your starting position again (Illus. 143). Then slide away to the outside and defend yourself to the right (Illus. 145). Your posture must be erect in the *kokutsu-dachi* (backwards) position in the defence with *shuto-uke*. In this position, your navel must point slightly upwards so that you can put force into your technique (by breathing) and keep your balance well.

Illus. 146. Nagashi-uke sweeps the attack away with an outside-inside motion.

Nagashi-uke or sweeping barrier (jodan and chudan)

This is a very good, rapid defence which requires little strength. The attacking arm is struck away from the outside to the inside with the surface of your hand (Illus. 146). When this is done, the defence can be directed against the outside or the inside of the attacking arm. It is suitable also as a defence against attacks on the face (*jodan-tsuki*).

Upper Level Defence (jodan)

Illus. 147. The rising X-block of juji-uke at the jodan level.

Juji-uke or upward or rising X-block

You learned this defence before in the downward direction. In the same way, you can also use it upwards or rising. When using it, keep your hands open. Lay your right hand over your left hand (Illus. 147). This defence requires relatively little strength. However, it is effective only when your elbows do not peek out on both sides of your body. (Reread the section on body tension, page 7.) A further advantage of this technique is that you can immediately grab with one or the other (or even both) hands and throw your opponent out of balance.

89

Illus. 148
Age-uke with fist.

Illus. 149
Age-uke with open hand.

Illus. 150. The Kareteka on the right is using age-uke with his fist to defend a blow at the jodan level.

Age-uke

Age-uke

Age-uke is the most commonly used defence for upper level attacks. The attacking arm is struck away in an upward direction, either with the fist (Illus. 148) or the open hand (Illus. 149). There is the characteristic twist of your wrist in this defence. In this, too, you use the outside bony edge of your lower arm (Illus. 150). When you come to a stop, your lower arm must be in front of your forehead. Turn your body to the side as you stop the blow. Do not allow your elbows to extend beyond the sides of your body. For this defence, your elbow must also be in a position directly above the middle of the thigh of your forward leg.

While this concludes the area of pure technique and its description, there are exercises you need to know for the defences and, following that, for the whole area of Karate technique.

For defending and counter-attacking:

You already know that turning your hip is the decisive factor in defending and counter-attacking. In the course of defending, your body is turned away; when you counter-attack turn it inward again. You must learn to turn your hip away and back again forcefully and obviously.

Types of exercise:

1. Continuous advancing in the *zenkutsu-dachi* (forward) position with a defence.

91

2. Continuous retreat in the *zenkutsu-dachi* position with a defence.

3. Continuous advancing in the *zenkutsu-dachi* position with a defence and an immediate counter-attack (*gyaku-zuki*).

4. Continuous retreat in the *zenkutsu-dachi* position with a defence and an immediate counter-attack (*gyaku-zuki*).

5. From *hachiji-dachi* (the basic position), retreat to the right in the *zenkutsu-dachi* position while defending to the left at the same time—then back to starting position. Then retreat to the left and defend to the right—and back to starting position. Now forward to the right and defend to the left. Then back and to the left.

6. The same thing, but with *gyaku-zuki* (the reverse punch) immediately following the defence. That is, always take one step backwards (right, left) and then forward. Always start from the *hachiji-dachi* position.

Advanced students can also practice the defences from the *kokutsu-dachi* (back stance) position, then turn inward to the *zenkutsu-dachi* position with *gyaku-suki*.

7. An exercise especially for the development of a hip turn: From *kiba-dachi* (straddle-leg stance), defend outwards to the front, with one arm defend with *gedan-uke* (turn the upper part of your body away with motion originating from the hip) and then counter-attack immediately with *gyaku-zuki*. Now defend with your other arm. Then with *soto-uke, uchi-uke, age-uke*. Always more to the right and to the left with an immediate counter-attack. This exercise is particularly valuable. It forces you to pay attention to turning your hips completely and consciously and develops the elasticity in your knees which you will need for every good Karate technique. This form of practice also requires little space and can be done very well at home. At the same time, if you leave out the foot movements, you can concentrate completely on turning your hips.

For defending with *shuto-uke* in connection with a counter-attack, usually the following forms are used:

Shuto-uke (edge-of-the-hand defence) in *kokutsu-dachi* (back stance). Place your leading leg the width of your shoulders to the side and rest on the ball of your foot into the *zenkutsu-dachi* (forward) position, then assume this position quickly. Immediately, counter-attack with *gyaku-zuki* (the reverse punch). The weight of your body, which is on your rear leg in the *kokutsu-dachi* position, is thrown forward by energetically straightening your bent rear leg. Thereby your counter-attack is intensified.

There is another very nice form of practice which develops hip turning in defence and counter-attack, and helps you to carry out the defences with a reflex action:

Both partners stand approximately a yard apart in the *hachiji-dachi* (basic) position. Then one partner strikes towards the face of his opponent with his fist, stopping short of course. The second partner defends with *age-uke* (rising blow at upper level), and then he strikes towards the face of his partner, who now also defends with *age-uke*.

Now the first partner strikes at the middle level and the defence is made with *soto-uke* (outer edge of lower arm). Then the second partner takes his turn, and finally the same thing is done with the lower level, where the defence used is *gedan-barai* (downward blow of lower arm).

Now you start over again from the beginning, doing the exercise continuously for some time. After a while, the execution of the defences will become more and more automatic and unconscious, a goal that is to be aimed at in the entire technique of Karate.

A coach can incorporate this exercise into regular gymnastics to great advantage.

Elasticity in your knees

When we considered *gyaku-zuki* (the reverse punch) in detail (page 34), we found that the rear leg must be elastic, that it should be relaxed and slightly bent, and that it is not tensed suddenly until the attack is made. This elasticity in your knees has a particular significance in connection with defending and counter-attacking. To be sure, the beginner is always taught that the position must always be correct, i.e., in the case of *zenkutsu-dachi* (forward position) that the rear leg must always be extended. How-

Illus. 151. The kiba-dachi position after defending with soto-uke. See the next page for your next move.

ever, the advanced student must be able to relax somewhat from this strict form in order to arrive at a mobile, effective technique. He must penetrate somewhat more deeply and understandingly into the matter.

In the case of *gyaku-zuki*, you soon learn that the force comes from your hips and your rear leg. Now, in connection with defending, the rear leg may bend somewhat when you turn your hips in the *zenkutsu-dachi* position. In the subsequent counter-attack, extend your leg energetically again and intensify its strength by doing this. (Reread under *gyaku-zuki* the exercise for the rear leg, page 39).

In other cases too, the advanced student must have elastic knees to make a technique most effective. For example, stand in the *kiba-dachi* position (Illus. 151). Perhaps you have escaped your opponent's attack this way or you have just defended with *soto-uke* from the inside.

If you want, for example, to attack with *yoko-empi-uchi* (elbow thrust to the side), you can only utilize the strength from your arm. (The *yoko-empi*, as you learned it, receives its force chiefly from the sideward advance of your body in the *kiba-dachi* position.) Since in this case you are already standing in the *kiba-dachi* position, the strength from your arm by itself will not make the *yoko-empi* very effective. Nevertheless, you know that the entire body should always participate in a good Karate technique. So, pull

94

Illus. 152	Illus. 153

Counter-attacking with drawn-back fist. Shift your center of gravity forward even though your feet don't change position.

back your fist and bend your entire body from the knees up. Then you strike out elastically. In this action, the center of gravity of your body is first displaced somewhat to your rear leg elastically by means of your knee (Illus. 151). Then you pull yourself together and throw your body forward again into the clean *kiba-dachi* position simultaneously with your attack (Illus. 152 and 153). By doing this you get your entire body behind the attack. When your attack reaches its goal, you have again assumed the *kiba-dachi* position. In other words, in the course of defending, you shift your weight (very elastically) to your rear leg (somewhat similar to the *kokutsu-dachi* or back position) and then throw it forward again elastically as you counter-attack going into the correct *kiba-dachi* position. This principle is also valid for *riken-uchi* (strike with the back of the fist), *tettsui-uchi* (side of the fist), and *haishu-uchi* (back of the hand) from the *kiba-dachi* position.

Practice this way: Stand in the *kiba-dachi* position and then reach out with *yoko-empi* to the left as you simultaneously shift your center of gravity slightly and elastically to your right leg. Then throw your body's center of gravity to the left again so that it is distributed on both legs at the same time as you use your technique for attacking your goal. Do the same thing to the right. Then perform *riken-uchi,* and so forth. This exercise develops elasticity in your knees, something which you must have if your Karate technique is to be good.

The speed and force of the techniques

Speed and force are always interrelated in a good Karate technique. You already know that Karate is nothing but speed transformed into force. However, swift motions are possible only when you are relaxed. Force alone (particularly powerful muscles, which precede force) cannot do it either. For Karate you need something that combines the two—speed and force.

In the section on body tension (page 7), you read that the person who masters his body tension is also master of relaxing his body. As far as Karate is concerned, you actually need both. Relaxation is important for the quick supple movements; the utmost tension is needed at the moment of striking.

The fibres of your muscles change their state of tension and contract simultaneously with every step you take and with every bend of your arms. Movements are possible because of this contraction of your muscles; this natural form of muscle movement is called "isotonic." If your limbs encounter resistance that prevents movement, then the fibres of your muscles do not contract in spite of great tension of your muscles. This form of muscle work without contraction at the same time is called "isometric," in the technical language of medicine.

During the 1920's, two scientists discovered that isometric tension of a muscle can strengthen it. They tied down one leg of a frog, but allowed him to move his other leg freely. The frog kept moving his free leg and struggling incessantly in the hope of getting himself free. After some time, the researchers observed that the muscles in the leg which had been fastened down were stronger than in the leg which had been trained by continuous motion. At that time, they were not able to explain this astonishing observation. Not until 1953 could the phenomenon be explained, after great progress had been made in the study of physiology of muscles, thanks to preliminary work of two Nobel prize winners, Otto Meyerhof and Archibald Vivian Hill. Not all muscle fibres in a bundle are called into play in the course of movements. Since most movements, such as those involved in physical work, are continuously repeated, the human body accustoms itself to using only part of the muscle fibres. In general, only about 60 per cent of the fibres are involved in working. It is different in the case of isometric tension. If resistance prevents the contraction of a muscle, then all its fibres are taxed. It has been determined that continuous contractions of the muscle fibres do not provide the stimulus for strengthening the musculature and the building of new fibres, but that tension alone is responsible for this.

Several years passed after 1953 until further details of muscle growth were clarified. Muscles develop best of all when they are tensed regularly, but only for the duration of a few seconds every time. A stimulus which lasts longer than 8 seconds does not encourage muscle growth. About 1960, the first exact instructions were worked out by muscle physiologists and sports physicians for isometric training according to a plan. It is interesting to note that I have found isometric exercises by the Japanese in an old English book on Jiu-jitsu. In addition, I found in a book about Okinawa Karate nothing other than the isometric exercises which science has discovered so recently.

There are a great many isometric exercises. Everyone can invent some by using his own imagination.

The only exercises of interest here are those which represent a particular advantage for Karate. The tension in Karate exists only for a short moment and at that point as many muscle fibres as possible should be tensed. Therefore, the isometrics should be chosen in such a way that exactly those groups of muscles are trained which are needed at the moment of striking.

This is exactly what our isometric exercises are aimed at. We exert resistance from the direction and counter-pressure in the direction that takes place in Karate movements. Some exercises for defence are illustrated as follows:

Isometric exercises to strengthen your arms.

Illus. 154—for *gedan-uke* (downward blow of lower arm).

Illus. 155—for *soto-ude-uke* (outer edge of lower arm, fist down).

Illus. 156—for *age-uke* (upward arm thrust).

Illus. 157—for *uchi-ude-uke* (inner edge of lower arm, fist down).

Illus. 158—for *shuto-uke* (edge of hand).

Illus. 159

Illus. 160

Practice in the *kiba-dachi* position, inhale, grab, and then exhale while exerting strong counter-pressure, and count to seven.

Exercises for attacking:

Illus. 159—for *kagi-zuki* (hook jab).

Illus. 160—for the blow with your fist.

Even more examples can be found with a little imagination, but those which are illustrated are sufficient.

Pointers:

If these exercises—which really do not take much time—are practiced regularly before every training session or at home, then you will very quickly notice a significant increase of force at the moment of striking. Also, you will develop great agility and speed in carrying out the individual techniques as a complementary effect of the exercise for tension.

For strengthening in general, you can invent a great many isometric exercises yourself. For example, press the palm of your hand against your forehead while exerting strong pressure in the opposite direction; press your palms against each other; press your linked hands against the back of your neck, and so on.

Illus. 161   Illus. 162   Illus. 163
Exercise borrowed from a Chinese master of Karate.

Here are a few strengthening exercises, especially valuable for Karate and Judo, which come from a Chinese master of Karate. They can be done very well with a belt, although originally practiced with a thick rope.

1. Grasp the belt as in Illus. 161. Go to the other side slowly after having tensed to your utmost while inhaling. Return while exhaling. This is one cycle. Practice it 6 times.

2. Illus. 162 and 163: Grasp and pull to the outside with both hands, inhale, and move your arms slowly downward. Then return upward again while exhaling. Practice 6 times.

Illus. 164   Illus. 165

3. Illus. 164 and 165: Put your foot into the belt loop and hold the ends with your extended hand. Inhale and draw it upward slowly against the counter-pressure of your foot. Exhale and return downwards slowly. Once again this forms a complete cycle. Practice 6 times.

These exercises can also be practiced while you are lying on the floor. Lie on your back when doing this. In the case of exercises 1 and 2, lift your extended legs approximately 4 inches from the floor (training for your stomach muscles). Lift the back of your neck while doing this. Continue to breathe in the same way in this position (breathe from the diaphragm). Exercise 1 can also be done while you lie on your stomach.

If all these exercises are carried out just once with great tension and counter-pressure, even a person who is athletically trained will have sore muscles the following day.

The exercises should not be practiced more than 6 times a day. The increase in your strength will be truly astonishing after you have practiced regularly for a short time. Judoka can also profit a great deal from these exercises.

Another good method to attain speed and force in attacking and defending is training with dumbbells. Use the small dumbbells weighing 1 to 3 pounds, which you can take in one hand.

To practice the blow with your fist:

1. Take a dumbbell in your right hand. Assume the starting position with your right hip. Your left hand, which is moving to the rear, is free. If you concentrate completely on the fact that your left hand moving to the rear determines your speed, and you move your hands back and forth quickly and forcefully, then the blow with your fist will also be quick and forceful. Do this exercise 10 times with the dumbbell in your right hand, then 10 times without the dumbbell. Then practice with the dumbbell in your left hand.

Hold dumbbells in both of your hands. Strike with alternate hands. Then strike a few times without the dumbbells.

Defences: Hold a dumbbell only in your defending hand as you go through the exercises for defence. If you are practicing in connection with *gyaku-zuki*, hold dumbbells in both hands. It is best to practice in the *kiba-dachi* position. After doing this, practice a few defences without dumbbells.

A basic principle: If you notice that you are getting slower and losing strength, put the dumbbells aside and practice briefly without dumbbells, quickly and forcefully.

Briefly, here is one more exercise which develops rapid force in the course of striking with your fist.

Stand in the *kiba-dachi* position with your elbows together approximately 4 inches away from your chest, your lower arms and fists together, and your fists at chin level (Illus. 166). From this position, strike blows with your fist, right and then left (Illus. 167), always springing back into the starting position again, with elbows together (Illus. 168). In this, you must aim for a shock effect within a very short distance. Be limber and relax when you practice. Concentrate the tension into the brief moment of striking, and spring back immediately again.

Here is another exercise which does not primarily serve to develop the technique of striking with your fist, but rather increases your endurance: Hold your fists closed loosely in front of your chest. Now strike with the *sanbon-renzuki* which is a triple blow—one upper level blow and two middle level blows. The tempo should be 1 . . . 2, 3. When doing this, the returning fist is brought back in front of your chest. Move naturally (walking around) and strike while you are moving. Do not strike with all your strength but only loosely. You should not strike with force until your breath and movements are co-ordinated. Practice for periods of 5 minutes.

A slight variation which takes somewhat more strength: Stand in the *kiba-dachi* position and strike with the complete *sanbon-renzuki*, i.e., the returning fist goes back to your hip in each case. Strike 600–900 times.

Here is a form of practice for striking with your fist which originated with the fighters from the southern provinces of the Chinese mainland who had "soft" fists: Set up a burning candle firmly at chest level. Stand in front of it in the *gedan-barai* defensive position and then strike quickly and forcefully with *gyaku-zuki*

Exercise to develop fist punching.

(reverse punch) toward the flame of the candle. The point at which you stop your blow should be approximately one inch from the flame. If your blow is loose and quick and comes to an exact stop, the flame will be extinguished by the air pressure. This is a very good exercise, but at the same time a very difficult one. You must be able to combine the soft with the hard. What is required and developed is lightning-fast loose striking and shock-like application of strength at an exactly defined point. This type of practice is usually not as much fun as breaking boards and tiles, striking at real obstacles (hitting posts, sandbags, horses) in order to harden your limbs. Some practitioners of Karate see only the hardness in it and do not understand that the real Karate fighter combines the hard with the soft in his character.

Practice striking toward the candle flame again and again. As you succeed increasingly frequently in "blowing out" the flame, and your movement is relatively effortless, you will have developed a far more dangerous blow with your fist than the person who develops callouses and cartilage at the *makiwara* (hitting post).

Less is more—I mean exercise with understanding and self-control.

One-minute training

This is a form of practice to be carried out at home. I was stimulated to make these experiments because, even after plenty of time, many of my beginning students did not execute the techniques cleanly. They were overwhelmed by the abundance of material to be learned, and they could no longer concentrate their controls on an individual technique when they were practicing. They divided their self-control, and to the same degree the effectiveness of their technique was diminished.

Now I assign "homework" for every day of the week. I undertake only one technique at a time, for example, *soto-uke* (see page 83). I show this technique in detail and explain it exactly. Then I assign the homework. Assume, for example, that this is Monday evening. The homework would be as follows:

For Tuesday: Stand in front of the mirror and carry out the movement of the *soto-uke* slowly and relaxed. Do this for one minute, alternately to the right and to the left.

For Wednesday: Do the same thing with increased self-control.

For Thursday: Continue to carry out the exercise slowly, but put force into the stopping point. Hold it for a second, breathe correctly.

For Friday: Do exactly the same thing with exact control of movement while doing it.

For Saturday: Begin slowly, then continually increase your speed while maintaining exact control.

For Sunday: Carry out the exercise quickly and forcefully.

Practice for just one minute in front of the mirror every day. You will have very good results from this concentrated practice for a week. You really need to practice for only one minute, but this must be completely concentrated. Concentration of effort impresses and imprints the correct execution of this technique and the correct succession of movements in your memory. Neverthe-

Illus. 169.
Class in
defence
practice.

less, this type of exercise should not be done for more than 5 minutes a day because, according to my experience, you no longer keep exactly to the exercise for the day in question, you go beyond it, or tire out your self-control. This "one-minute training," along with the other exercises to be done at home, is especially recommended for advanced students.

All the basic techniques, as they have been described, are practiced in the basic school, the Karate *dojo* or *kihon*. All the pupils line up in rows behind each other according to the colors of their belts, the highest *kyu* or grades to the right facing the instructor. The exercises are practiced by orders (counting) or by the individuals while the instructor (*sensei*) walks by and checks.

It is now absolutely necessary for the advanced Karateka, who

105

Illus. 170. A class in the sei-za or tai-za position learning correct breathing. This position, resting on heels, allows you to be completely relaxed.

has mastered the individual techniques, to get a feeling of what it is like when a technique strikes and hits its goal with full force. In practicing attacks into empty air, the student cannot get close to the real thing. To overcome this, there is a piece of apparatus called the *makiwara*. This is basically a post which has been wrapped with straw, against which all arm and foot techniques can be practiced. This practice apparatus serves to harden your limbs. Other equipment includes the sandbag for hand and foot techniques, and the horse, an apparatus found in every gym, which is especially suitable for foot techniques. The horse can also be used like a *makiwara*.

With the apparatus you can practice the application of force for the *mae-geri-ke-komi* and *yoko-geri-ke-komi*. Start from all positions—advancing, starting from a turn, and so forth. Doing this will also develop a good eye and how to estimate distance correctly.

A further aid in Karate training is scheduling regular sessions of running. If you force yourself to do this regularly and, if possible, alone, you will soon develop something of the "fighting spirit" you need in Karate. When you run alone, always force yourself to endure even more than if someone were running with you.

However, do not exaggerate at the beginning, but build up to this slowly.

A further exercise which is excellent for learning correct breathing is sitting in the *sei-za* (or *tai-za*) position (Illus. 170). Sit on your heels completely relaxed with the upper part of your body erect (your navel must point slightly upwards). Breathe with your diaphragm. While you are doing this, always be conscious of the middle of your body, the *hara*. Look straight ahead at some point and do not think of anything definite, but rather let thoughts fly through your mind like a breeze. This exercise, if carried out regularly, will also influence your inner attitude very beneficially. However, we will go further into this later.

One of the most important prerequisites for learning true Karate is following a sensible way of life: Moderation in smoking and drinking, sufficient sleep, moderate stimulation (avoid too many movies, too much television and spectator sports). Only a person with a healthy body and mind is capable of concentrating and really learning Karate.

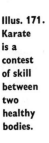

Illus. 171. Karate is a contest of skill between two healthy bodies.

Illus. 172

Illus. 173

Back step into gedan-gamae, then forwards into oi-zuki, while your opponent defends with soto-uke.

6. Contest Exercises
(Kumite)

Up to this point we have only examined the techniques of Karate. Whenever you had a partner, the purpose of his presence was to help you with your exercises. However, Karate is primarily a contest between two fighters. You are confronted by an opponent against whom you must defend yourself and counter-attack. In other words, the basic techniques of this sport are dominated by the knowledge that you are training for an actual Karate combat.

There are various contest (or *kumite*) forms (or *katas*) of exercise:

1. *Kihon-kumite* (basic partner training)
   a) *ippon-kumite*
   b) *sanbon-* and *gohon-kumite*
2. *Jiyu-ippon-kumite* (semi-free sparring)
3. *Jiyu-kumite* (free-style contest)

The main purpose of the contest exercises in *kihon-kumite* and in *jiyu-ippon-kumite* is to train your precision and your eye. Constant training will teach you reflex-conditioned reactions, inducing within you a sense of caution and care. Ideally, in the end you will hardly have to think about these movements and can almost shut out your conscious concentration on them. This ideal state can only be achieved by persistent training. In *kihon-kumite* every attack and every defence is precisely thought out beforehand. Your unconscious precision and your exactitude is developed for use in a free contest.

Ippon-kumite

The partners confront each other in *hachiji-dachi*, the basic position. One partner, the attacker, assumes a distance, i.e., he stretches out both arms (making fists) until they touch his partner's chest. Now he steps back with his right foot (Illus. 172) in the position called *gedan-gamae*. Then he attacks on the right with *oi-zuki* (Illus. 173), for instance at the middle level (announcing it beforehand). His partner turns and steps back with his right foot, defends himself in the process with *soto-uke* (Illus. 173), and in turn counter-attacks with *gyaku-zuki* on the right (Illus. 174).

The announcement by the instructor would sound something like this: Attack *oi-zuki* (simultaneous jab same side), middle

Illus. 174. From a defensive soto-uke, the Kareteka on the right is counter-attacking with gyaku-zuki.

Illus. 175
Soto-uke from inside.

Illus. 176
Counter-attack with shito-uke.

level. Defend *soto-uke* from the outside. Counter-attack *gyaku-zuki*. Of course, it is also possible to defend yourself from inside (back to left and a left defence) or at a right angle, either moving back to left or right and from inside (Illus. 175) or defending yourself from outside with *soto-uke*. You can also counter-attack *empi-uchi* (with elbow), *shuto-uchi* (Illus. 176), *yoko-geri*, etc. It is imperative that you exercise the *kihon-kumite* in as many variations as possible, but precisely and forcefully. Mainly you should make sure that the attacking arm and attacking leg of your partner are hit by your defensive measures before your own attacking limbs are stretched out (and thus frozen). There are two reasons for this:

1. If you wait to be struck by the attacking limbs at the very moment when they are fully stretched, this is precisely the moment when the strike is at its most awesome strength. In order to push or strike the assaulting limb aside, you would need enormous strength.

2. Still more important: If you defend yourself only at the moment when the opponent's attack is at its most powerful, when the limbs are fully stretched and "frozen," your defence will come too late. Timing is decisive.

Consequently you have to be faster with your defence than your opponent with his attack. Always anticipate your opponent's movements. Your opponent's attacking leg or arm must be struck while they are still in motion and "unfrozen." Then your defence will be much more effective and you can knock aside any blow regardless of force.

Sanbon- and gohon-kumite

When performing these exercises your partner attacks three times or five times in a row, either at your middle or upper level. Retreating, you must defend yourself three or five times and after the last attack lead into a forceful counter-attack. Then you are the attacker and the whole procedure is reversed. This exercise demands that your thrusts be speedy, exact and powerful and simultaneously that you take care not to lose your balance. Your partner defending himself must see to it that he repulses your attack with precision.

Beginners must train themselves step by step, with clean and precise movements, attacking and aiming with precision, and defending themselves in like manner.

Sanbon and, more importantly, *gohon* contests are of great significance for the advanced student. The defender must always be able to follow the movements of the attacker as if he were himself an extension of the attacker. When the attacker stops, the defender must also halt his movements on the spot. When the attacker advances, the defender must move back the same distance, if possible without delay. As long as you keep a certain distance from your opponent throughout the contest you should be safe. The importance of this series of movements cannot be stressed enough.

Therefore, advanced students should always continue to exercise *gohon-kumite*, of course with a slight variation from the novice: movements of advance and retreat should be speedier and more fluid. Infuse these motions with intensified force. As the attacker, increase the effort of your assaults until the last thrust becomes the most powerful. The same applies to the defence. You will soon anticipate the movements of your opponent. You can learn to recognize the intent of your partner the very moment he starts

Illus. 177 (left). A class in Karate is practicing contest techniques. The left row is showing gedan-gamae while the right row remains in hachiji-dachi. Illus. 178 (right). As the left row attacks with zuki at the chudan (middle) level, the right row defends with soto-uke (outer edge of forearm).

to attack you. And this is precisely the aim of the ultimate free contest. You should reach the point where you can sense the attack your partner is planning, not only so that you can prepare yourself, but so that you can anticipate the force and nature of the attack. You should train yourself to such an ideal state that you can "smell out" the attack and react to it automatically without consciously thinking about it or your defensive measures.

Jiyu-ippon-kumite

A further step on the path to this goal is this semi-free sparring form in which the two partners move freely and in all directions as in a free-style contest. Who is to be the attacker and who the defender is decided prior to the contest, as is the form of the attack (for example, *oi-zuki*—lunge punch, same side—middle level). The attacker has to find an opening and gain the right distance from his opponent before the attack begins. The defender has to wait for the attack and be prepared to defend himself immediately. As soon as the attack starts, he must ward it off or evade it and go into a counter-attack. As a result, the roles reverse and the attacker becomes defender. This type of exercise makes great demands on the Karateka. It is an excellent exercise to find the right distance, both in the offensive and defensive stances. The lightning-quick recognition and exploitation of an opening in your opponent's cover will become second nature, as should the quick and forceful application of those techniques which follow from the opponent's movement.

A form of the *jiyu-ippon-kumite* which is still more challenging is the variation in which only the attacker and defender are appointed, and not the form of attack. Before proceeding to the free-style contest a few observations regarding the fighting postures are in order with special emphasis on *jiyu-ippon-kumite* and *jiyu-kumite*.

Contest positions

No contest stance or position is required. You can choose the positions most advantageous to your attack or defence. Stances with tensed muscles are not suitable for these purposes since they prevent effective reflex action and quick movement. Such motions are—as you have seen before—only possible when your muscles are relaxed. Your stance must be loose and natural. Don't move more than necessary. (Illus. 179 and 180 on next page.)

For an attack during *jiyu-ippon-kumite* and *jiyu-kumite*:

Always start out with a "long" attack, i.e., throw the weight of your body behind your punch, leaning forward. These exercises are useful when performing *ippon-kumite* and *sanbon-* and *gohon-kumite*. Catapult yourself all the way to the fore when attacking. When your defending partner does not step back far enough you should be able to break through his defences. You can even deal him such a heavy blow that he falls to the ground (provided that your forward movement emanates from the *hara*).

During the *jiyu-ippon-kumite* go on the offensive as if you intend

Illus. 179. The contest begins but the stance must stay loose and natural.

to hit your opponent. You must concentrate on breaking through with your attack or else your Karate will be unrealistic. Only when you notice that your partner defends himself too late, or not at all, is it time for you to stop so that he is not hit. This is to point out that the correct *jiyu-ippon-kumite* and, of course, especially the *jiyu-kumite* (free-style contest) make great demands on the ability and precision of your technique, and on your unconscious yet assured reflexes—characteristics which can only be achieved by persistent and uncompromising training.

The same principle of the "long attack" is also applicable to the leg-attack. Here, too, your *hara*, your whole body, must be thrown forward. This helps to lend greater force and thrust to

Illus. 180. Practice contest techniques in the gym until you are certain you are attacking with your whole body, your hara.

114

your attack as well as enable you to take the offensive from a greater and safer distance. In this way, a weak defence can be easily broken. Moreover, even if you should fail to penetrate your opponent's defences with such a leg assault, it still might enable you to come closer to him and to continue the contest without delay by applying your hand techniques. Consequently, there is this basic principle to be remembered in a contest: that in Karate techniques every part of your body has to participate. The starting point and the source of your strength for full-body movements always is the *hara*.

For the free-style contest remember these principles:

Never attack with your arms and legs only, but always employ your whole body (*hara*).

In a free-style contest, only advanced students are welcome.

7. The Contest

Jiyu-kumite, the free-style contest

Illus. 181–184 show positions in a contest.

This is the apex of Karate. But it is a stage reserved only to the Karateka who is willing to apply himself with diligence and tenacity to the hard school of precision and exactness. When performing in a free-style contest, every participant must be in the position to avert and stop even the most powerful of attacks shortly before it reaches its target. Although the path to this final form advances step by step (*kihon*: basic steps; *kihon-kumite*: basic partner exercises; *jiyu-ippon-kumite*: semi-free sparring; *jiyu-kumite*: free-style contest), there are possibilities that you can

Illus. 183. The back kick, ushiro-geri.

take a short-cut and start earlier. Karate is an organic entity and the feeling for this should be aroused in each student starting with his first lesson.

Here are a few preparation exercises for your contest:

You have learned positions and movements, as well as the most important defences and counter-attacks, *oi-zuki* and *gyaku-zuki*. Henceforth whenever you train, carry out your basic partner contest-exercises (*kihon-kumite*). Naturally, at first, your individual techniques will not be imbued with great strength, your movements will lack the necessary speed. But as time progresses, so will you and your exercises. Once you avert and defend yourself against

Illus. 184. The roundhouse kick, mawashi-geri.

Practice for the contest.

an attack, and repulse it with a counter-attack, this will give you a feeling for keeping the right distance from your opponent. It will also prove that you can defend yourself and counter-attack.

Here is another exercise you can begin now: Follow the contest position, the cover, and then place yourself opposite your partner for the contest. Move in a manner befitting the Karateka, i.e., economically, yet lightning-quick. Should your opponent advance on you with a large or sliding step, react at once by moving back still faster. Pay attention to your balance and tense your muscles the moment both feet settle down again on the floor. Keep the upper part of your body upright. It is quite possible that both of you will simultaneously attack and collide. Put up your cover at once and push yourself from your opponent. At this juncture, do not attack or go over to the defence. The exercise itself will help you to develop your Karate movements for the next step in the contest.

This next step would be the *jiyu-ippon-kumite*. Your training for definitive movements and exactness must run concurrently, as when performing in *kihon-kumite*. This point is important to remember: Despite your early contest exercises, never relax in applying your basic and elementary Karate principles. These form the background to everything in this sport. Your progress finally depends on the basic Karate foundation you have developed for yourself.

A few more hints for the free-style contest: Wait until you see an opening in your opponent's cover, then take advantage of it and attack him. You may even induce your opponent to drop his cover:

1. Attack actively by feigning an attack and exploiting the opening in his cover which he drops as a result of his defence-reaction. For instance: (a) Aim your first fist attack at his face. Your opponent will raise his hands in defence and the fist of your other hand will proceed with the real attack, driving home on his solar plexus. Or (b) apply *mae-geri* (forward kick with your foot) to his solar plexus. Your opponent will lower his arms in defence, and you thrust your leg as far forward as possible with a simultaneous *oi-zuki* (pursuit blow) to his face.

2. Attack *passively*: This time you pretend to drop your defences. This will tempt your opponent to proceed with an attack on you. You have waited for this and when it comes, you evade it or defend yourself and go over to a strong counter-attack. This form of contest technique conforms to the true essence of Karate, but it demands great agility and skill, a well-trained eye and a reflex-conditioned self-assurance both in defence and counter-attack.

This is another exercise for the contest which will school you in your unconscious reflex reaction: Form a circle about 5 to 6 yards in diameter with four men standing outside and one inside of it. Only one man may stay inside this circle. The four men on the outside each try to deal a blow to the inside-man's shoulder without the latter observing it. Should one succeed, the man who dealt the blow enters the circle while the other joins the rank of the men outside. The man inside the circle has to recognize the "attacks" at the right time and ward them off with a Karate attack. If he is able to apply a well-aimed strong assault, the outside man against whom it was directed must be removed from the circle. Of course the man on the outside should exert every effort to defend himself against the man inside the circle and still deal the blow to the insider's shoulder. This exercise is only suitable for advanced students with an excellent record in Karate.

A valuable and beautiful form of exercise for the Karate contest is provided by training (*jiyu-ippon-kumite* and *jiyu-kumite*) out-of-doors. The ground does not necessarily have to be even. In the countryside you can select a spot which appears most advantageous to you. It is up to your opponent then to attack you. In this fashion, both partners learn to stand on difficult terrain for attack and defence.

Another hint for contest exercises: If you decide to attack with *oi-zuki* and stand too far away for a sliding step, pull back your front leg behind the other leg by about 12 inches (leaving the weight of your body in front) and propel yourself with one leg to the fore as fast as you can. This attack will come as a great surprise to your opponent.

The next aspect of Karate can only be learned from personal instruction.

8. The Kata

In the *kata* (Illus. 185) a number of pre-determined defences and attacks are conducted in a fixed order of succession to demonstrate methods of defence, attack and counter-attack. There are about 50 of such *kata*, most of which originated in ancient times. Until about 30 years ago, the *kata* was considered the ideal form of Karate. Only since then have the *kumite* forms and *jiyu-kumite* been developed. Even today Karate championships are divided in two parts: *Kata* tournaments (*kata-shiai*) and contest tournaments (*kumite-shiai*).

In the case of *kata-shiai*, contest evaluators assess the performances of the individual, rather like referees in a figure-skating contest. The overall impression of the individual is appraised, and this is determined by the suppleness of movements, the force and precision of techniques, the dynamics of the entire flexible performance.

Kata is usually required of beginners. Some Karateka regard these exercises as a necessary evil for acquiring their black belts. However, a beautifully executed *kata* always arouses the enthusiasm

of the spectators for its aesthetic and mobile appeal. The harmony of the motions and the explosive dynamics of the exhibition give the onlookers, as well as the Karateka, a feeling of tremendous satisfaction. But this sense of delight and rapture is only shared by spectators and participants alike provided the *kata* is displayed as an organic whole. Only by attaining this goal can a performance really "live." So, whoever views the *kata* as nothing more than a separated unconnected series of exercises has completely missed the essential point.

The positions and movements and individual techniques must be mastered in all their totality of strength and precision. The *kata* can, for this reason, be considered excellent basic training for the development of good Karate technique: balance, self-assured movements, forceful attacks, precise defences—all these will be improved. No substitute serves as well for the elementary basis of contest training. Since in performing a *kata* several imaginary partners must be attacked and defended against from all directions (Illus. 186), this aspect provides a great proving ground for the application of various techniques in a number of situations and indirectly serves as fine training for the free contest.

However, back to our earlier stipulation: A correct *kata* is an organic whole, not just a joining together of several perfectly executed techniques. This in turn provides us with a few plain hints for our instruction in *kata*.

An organic entity is not something knotted together, but something growing out of a preceding movement. Therefore, beginners should learn the lessons of *kata* before they have mastered the various techniques down to the last iota of perfection and exactitude. Important is the totality of the performance. The sharpening up of the separate techniques will come as time progresses. Any *kata* so acquired will soon assume the essence of "life." Once this lesson has penetrated and become second nature to you, you will not get stuck in the execution of your performance. After all, the subconscious control over your movements is projected in the display of your *kata*.

When you master this predetermined course of movements with almost somnambulistic assurance, you will have gradually

**Illus. 187.
Practice for the kata may look like a dance in a trance.**

absorbed still another aim of Karate: the exhibition of motions and techniques instinctively with trancelike confidence (Illus. 187).

Therefore, never neglect your *kata*! Make an effort to add as much as possible to this by training constantly.

Here are two more exercises for the *kata*: For muscular coordination of the arm, perform your *kata* exercises with dumbbells in your hands; for a strong foundation of the lower part of your body, place a partner on your shoulders and perform all movements and steps of the *kata* this way. After this, reverse the roles.

Once more, do you still pay attention to the fact that your navel must always point slightly up? And that the *hara* serves as the middle of your body? Do you still remember the correct way to brace yourself and tense your muscles as well as to relax by breathing?

9. The Spiritual Basis of Karate

We have now completed the discussion of pure Karate techniques. It is not the end of your learning. This is really the starting point —something we will prove in a little while.

At first a few observations regarding Karate's history: Karate is a Japanese name and means literally "Empty unarmed hand." It is interesting that this art is by no means Japanese in origin as might be suspected from the name. On the contrary, this sport has been known in Japan only since the early 1900's. It was formally introduced to Japan by Gichin Funakoshi, a citizen of Okinawa. On that island, Karate, which originated in China, was fully developed. Ironically, we have to thank the Japanese conquerors of Okinawa in the late 19th century, for they would not allow Okinawan natives to carry arms, forcing them to circumvent the edict by devising and mastering a form of contest without arms.

Furthermore, it is interesting to note that all over Southeast Asia there are many systems of pugilism. The "great-grandfather" of all of these contests is the Chinese form of fisticuffs or boxing, which is still being practiced today in China under the names of "Chuang fa" or "Kung fu" and in China and elsewhere under the name of "Kempo." Karate is simply the best known of these systems. Nevertheless we owe our gratitude to the Japanese for having brought this sport into full bloom.

Let us take a look at the motto of the Japanese Karate Association and adopt it for our own:

"The primary aim in the art of Karate is neither victory nor defeat—the true Karate contestant strives for the perfection of his character."

This proverb shows that the essence of Karate is neither mastering the technique of this sport nor victory over your opponent, but triumph over yourself. It follows that the true nature of Karate serves as a school for life.

"But," you will protest, "doesn't this presuppose that the above words 'to strive for' imply that the student must have good will? What happens then when someone with criminal intentions learns the techniques of this sport?"

To this objection it is best for you to recall: The first things a Karateka must learn are the positions which, to be honest, are and look clumsy and do not make much sense at first. Next follows the rather dull learning period of the various techniques in *kihon* (basic training). This always proves to be a hard course. You have to conquer yourself constantly. You have to concentrate, to approach the techniques with deep understanding and practice incessantly and self-critically. This by itself requires great will power. Such training demands and develops certain characteristics: concentration, an alert mind, will power, self-control, all of which will stand you in good stead throughout life. Karate therefore really is a school preparing you for the challenges in life. All this becomes obvious after a few lessons in this sport. Experience has fortunately shown that when criminal characters are intent on learning the art of Karate with the sole purpose of using the techniques for offensive reasons, they miss the entire point of the basic schooling. For months on end they are not shown "lethal blows" but rather subjected to "senseless" and "awkward" positions and movements. In most cases such scoundrels drop out after several weeks. They don't have the stamina to train themselves.

It is worthwhile to point out once more at this juncture that in a truly understood Karate lesson no real danger exists. It takes a long time to attain ability in Karate.

Learning true Karate (as well as Judo and other contest sports) is of great value. With the aid of a conscientious and responsible instructor, Karate can serve as the backbone for a wholesome outlook on life. It can truly be of great service in your attempt to perfect your character. Naturally, if you do not stick to it and use your will power, you will not prevail. I have discovered, to my great and pleasant surprise that in the course of oral instructions I have given as well as during the period of physical training, many of my students have found within their natures unsuspected reservoirs of will power.

Starting with your first schooling, Karate demands a thorough understanding of and reflection on the psychological reality and regulations of the sport, and furthermore persistent, self-critical training governed by the motto, "Less is more," correctly understood. The characteristics and experiences you gain will be of special value in meeting the requirements of your daily life if you truly understand your Karate lessons and apply them to life. Once your mind no longer has to concentrate consciously on individual movements and techniques, your mind can be considered free, prepared for the challenges of the contest. Only by performing the totality of your motions almost as if "in a trance" can you be certain that your mind is capable of applying your actions with a well-nigh effortless confidence to any given situation. This achievement will imbue you with confidence under all circumstances. You know that regardless of how your opponent attacks, you are in control of all your defences. This inner equanimity—and healthy self-assurance—will prove most rewarding in any situation that might arise in life.

A person matures as he goes through life. Anyone struggling upward over life's obstacles without breaking or capitulating is composed, intelligent and endowed with an inner superiority. Karate looks at these aims as its final goal to be emulated: by perseverance in conquest over your weakness (during the elementary training period) and later in contest with your partner (*kumite*) to aspire to this essential philosophy of life. A person who does not struggle, who does not mentally or psychologically grapple with happenings or things that challenge him day by day has lost something of his human psyche.

Illus. 188. Taiji Kase, 6th Dan, one of Karate's highest ranking exponents.

This is part of today's sickness. Young people often do not know what to do with themselves, bored as they may be. They plunge from one superficial pastime into another and often end up regarding themselves as pathetic and bored failures. All you have to do is to look at the blank faces in a bar or an amusement arcade where youngsters hang out. The point that strikes you at once is that these youths don't want to do anything on their own—they want to be entertained. When it comes to intelligent conversation or discussion (a contest between minds), they exhibit a complete absence of sensible and meaningful talk.

"Stagnation means boredom, death; aspiration means life." We could be heartless and maintain that the life many people (and by no means merely young people) lead is not really a life for humans, but sheer vegetation, almost inhuman. They think of today, never bother about tomorrow. Their leisure lacks goals, is aimless wandering. Their joy lies in nihilism rather than in the hope for a constructive future.

Against all these attitudes, Karate stands as a philosophy which can help anyone to master life with an inner wholesomeness.

Life is a struggle and only in struggling do humans grow and mature. It is not difficult to understand what the Greek philosopher Heraclitus meant when he said that "War is the father of all things." Along the same line, with a never-rest-on-your-laurels argument, runs Goethe's adage in "Faust" when he has the angels utter the line: "Whoever strives and struggles, him we can liberate."

Once Taiji Kase, 6th Dan (Illus. 188), told me: "Karate is not a shallow sport. You can always probe deeper into it but will never be able to completely plumb its depths." And yet there are many students who claim they know all about Karate once they have managed to master a few of the techniques!

So be cautious! With the mastery of these techniques, only then does the real Karate start. Only then can your mind be truly free, liberated from the conscious clutter of movements. When you have automatic self-assurance and control over your body movements, then you can gain mental and spiritual serenity, adjust completely to life. If you are prepared to take this seriously, then Karate (Judo, etc.) will not only serve as a means to defend yourself in an emergency but, more importantly, as a way to police the physical and mental aspects of your personality. In the final analysis, consequently, you not only defeat your opponent but the weaknesses in yourself.

When you learn to drive a car, your entire attention and concentration at first is focused on various activities: shifting of gears, operating the clutch, brake, and steering wheel; when you first learn to dance you count 1–2–3, step to the left, etc. It is only later, after you have mastered the art of driving or dancing, that you can perform these duties and at the same time converse and joke with your backseat driver or dancing partner. The techniques of braking and the counting of steps have become second nature to you. This is how it should be with your Karate. When your mind has been liberated of technique, it is freed to act subconsciously.

The psyche is like water (misu no kokoro)

The mind should be calm, like a surface of a village pond—serene and ready to ebb away gradually whenever and wherever it is needed. The mirror of the pond's surface reflects everything surrounding it. Thus, you are able to absorb the reflected intent of your opponent; your mind is at your disposal and lets you react instinctively. This swift reaction should relate to all situations, but it is only possible if your mind gets "stuck" nowhere and remains as serene as the water in the pond. What you need is absolute calm and concentration. If your mind swerves for only one second, or fixes upon one aspect only, or if it deliberately occupies itself with, for example, the possibility of an attack, then you may be surprised by a completely unexpected attack from your opponent, merely because your mind was not calm and ready—but was burdened. It was, so to speak, disturbed, just like the ruffled waters of a lake. You know that when the surface of water is rippled by waves it can no longer reflect its surroundings.

Remove yourself at once from any uneasy attitudes. Call the ideal state equanimity if you will. To achieve this state, you will have to train yourself. The novice must practice his techniques with persistent concentration. Even the experts can only retain their mastery of these techniques by continuing their practice year after year. Their minds have to remain free, calm, unencumbered and ready, just like the water of a still pond.

Through years of conscientious training you will attain the exhilarating sensation of self-liberation. You will hardly be aware of the defensive or offensive measures you are using and can adapt yourself to any situation without losing your "cool."

"Due to his self-consciousness Man is frequently converted into a creature of automation," writes E. Hoelker in "Doctor and Sport, the German Medical Weekly." When you no longer fix your thoughts upon a single aim, when you aspire to nothing, want and expect nothing, yet when you know how to utilize your unswerving strength to achieve the possible as well as the impossible—this attitude, because of its unpremeditated and selfless nature, is considered by many masters of Karate as being on the elevated plateau called "spiritual." The mind is saturated with spiritual alertness and is consequently referred to as "correct presence of mind." The mind is ubiquitous, simply because it does not stick to one particular spot, but is everywhere.

A mind is like the moon (tsuki no kokoro)

Moonlight can be seen everywhere, yet it clings nowhere. In like manner you must be conscious of the movements of your opponent; that is, you must be like the moon which looks upon everything yet does not cling to any one spot. Nervousness or the slightest distraction and intimidation resemble the clouds which move in front of the moon.

Naturally you can apply this philosophy to every situation in life, deploying your reservoir of equanimity for each event and using your mental attitude for the correct handling of things. The source and the nature of this mental attitude is *hara* for the Japanese.

The mind may be able to discover an opening in your opponent's stance, but this will be of little avail to you if you lack the will to exploit this situation at once.

General observations about the contest

A lesson you have learned previously is that actual fighting and defence cannot be considered so much a technical as a psychological problem. The best technique, the finest know-how, will let you down if you are not in full control of yourself.

Here are a few reflections which, like earlier ones, not only apply to Karate but to all forms of dual sports. In the chapter dealing with contest positions you were asked to keep your body as loose, limp, relaxed and natural as possible, yet be prepared for all eventualities. "Anyone who is truly prepared does not appear to be prepared at all." You must not show preparedness in the slightest degree although you must be ready for everything.

It is told of old masters of sword fights that throughout the day they moved in such a way as *never* to expose themselves to attack through an opening in their deportment. This of course is the ideal aim for every student of a contest sport: to reach a state of such perfection that your instincts guide you through daily life with a sense of preparedness for all situations.

Your eyes should always level with the eyes of your opponent. The eye is the mirror of the soul. You can thus look "into" your partner and even influence his mental attitude through your own, as reflected in your eyes. Concurrently with this, you can survey each movement of his arms, legs, etc.

The real fighter does not want to fight. He does not ponder victory or defeat. He does not mix in fights, except when an innocent person is in dire need or danger. As long as he hankers after fisticuffs and consciously concentrates only on triumphing over his opponent, he is not fully in possession of the "mind of the water." His mind is too preoccupied and fixed on one direction and, as a result, is not free.

The hara

Now, back to the meaning of *hara*, the focal point of the body, the center of gravity of man, just below the navel. You have already learned about the technical aspects of *hara*, as in posture and breathing. But *hara* also has more meaningful implications.

The end result of our life struggle—as of the true Karate—should be attaining an inner posture or attitude. This attitude is the consequence of your maturing. It means that you have found your crucial point. The symbol of this point is *hara*. It is this concept, this frame of mind, from which all things originate and to which all things return. This spiritual center of gravity relates to the center of gravity of the body, and an understanding of this proves that you have discovered your spiritual as well as physical center. The physical center is the *hara*. The inner posture of a sitting Japanese is as meaningful to him as is his visible posture. The Japanese consequently finds a relaxed yet upright calm within him in all situations of life.

The unifying words, "upright" and "relaxed" are characteristic of this attitude. You will find yourself inwardly completely harmonized and balanced. Upright, cool, steadfast and collected—these are the signs, the characteristics of this spirito-mental posture. The Japanese regards victory in the sense of relating his existence to the total expression of *hara*. Thus, how you stand and sit, so will you walk and dance and act and wrestle. In the same fashion you must also fight "without motion," because every movement is, so to speak, anchored to the immovable center of gravity (the *hara*) from which all movements spring and derive their strength, direction and degree of control.

Once you have discovered the secret of *hara* for yourself, you are no longer so dependent on physical exertion, but can win with a completely different sort of force. *Hara* hides an almost super-natural strength which will inspire you to extraordinary feats of accomplishments in daily life. And since *hara* forms a subconscious background in the everyday life activities of the Japanese, serving them as a basis of inner maturity, they can take advantage of this mysterious strength and draw from it at will to achieve enormous feats in mental and physical performance. With *hara* you keep your presence of mind, in deed and otherwise. Those in possession of *hara* are prepared for every situation, even death. They can bow before the victor, in humility and without shame, and they have the patience to wait.

When you read about practicing, you will think of these actions that help you to master your sport. You will want to perfect your techniques and tactics. Practicing over and over again carries the seed of eventual perfection, which in its turn can help you to become a master, a champion. But the self-confidence that backs your attainments depends on more than merely a perfected ability to do something. Otherwise all you can be said to master is the technique of a thing; you will not have truly mastered yourself.

For instance, if you are easily distracted or intimidated, all your learned techniques and ability will forsake you at a decisive moment.

To exert complete control over yourself requires special practice and this is not just the result of technical know-how, but of your inner character development. In this sort of practice there is no visible effort, but change within. Your mind should not take aim for physical victory but for inner gain.

You will now be able to understand what the Japanese means when he says: "Shooting with an arrow and dancing, decorating with flowers and singing, drinking tea and wrestling—it is all the same." Literally, or visually, this adage has little meaning. No— the Japanese artist aims for the totality of the experience and acting it out. The consequence is that the effort will be child's play and the achievement somehow the result of an inner effortless instinct. Allegorically, this is almost like a tree shedding a ripe apple without being conscious of it. The nucleus of this mental attitude is the imperturbability of the center of gravity in the *hara*. If you recognize the truth of all this, you will be able to conquer yourself and your weaknesses and develop your character. Of course, you must set your mind to the task and draw on your faculties of concentration, your will power and alertness.

The actual *hara* can therefore begin only after the techniques have been learned and become second nature. Plainly, this automatic execution of exercises has an additional value. Ego-fixation can be made to retire, because only if an egotistical attitude no longer plays a major role in your life can perfection and achievement come to its fullest bloom. Comprehending this rule will give you a clearer understanding of the possibilities and strength of yourself, and subsequently help in the execution of every form of activity. In a cultivated *hara*, you are the owner of and master over uncommon strength and dependable precision to perform actions which, failing this *hara*, not even the most perfect skill, the hardest will or the most alert attention could bring about. "Total perfection is possible only with *hara*."

You will develop a number of characteristic faculties by practicing *hara*: Total serenity (equanimity and self-possession), yet at the same time a higher sensitivity and comprehension, as well as a preparedness for every surprise and a capacity for lightning-quick decisions which demand hard-headed judgments.

It is not easy to defeat a person with *hara*, but even if you are knocked down with hard blows, your *hara* will swing you back safely on your feet in no time. *Hara* is your firm anchor, which always enables you to find your "center of gravity" again.

But how can you actually practice the *hara*?

Although we have briefly touched on this problem while discussing the various techniques, let us probe a bit deeper into this most important aspect of Karate.

Stand absolutely relaxed and let your shoulders droop. Prepare the lower part of your abdomen for an opponent's thrust without being overly tense. Just let this thought go through your mind: "I am strong. I feel an important part of myself in this lower region, just below the navel." Once you have accepted this concept you will feel quite different, inwardly released and relaxed, upright and serene.

The decisive factor for the attainment of this is equalization of the concepts of tension and relaxation within yourself.

Combined with this concept, of course, is correct breathing.

Illus. 189. The tai-za position, the best for practicing breathing.

Your breathing, under the right controls, comes from your diaphragm. Be quite conscientious about the practicing of your breathing. Practice while sitting down and best of all in the *tai-za* position (Illus. 189). Persisting in this exercise will help you to find your way to practicing *hara*. Sit like this every day for half an hour, inhale and exhale with your diaphragm and put some strength in your abdominal region. Breathe through your nose and keep your mouth closed. Exhale very slowly, but not all the way, so that you can still utter a few words without having to inhale. As you exhale, try to add some strength to your abdomen. When you inhale do it in one brief heave. Yet never force your breathing, let it flow peacefully. As time progresses, you will be able to breathe like this about 10 times per minute; do not attempt to do more; in fact, if you can cut down on the number of exhalations per minute, so much the better. Soon you will reach the point where your respiration flows quite smoothly, almost instinctively. This is an indication that you are well on the way to developing your *hara* fully.

It goes without saying that *hara* must be performed in every posture. Regardless of whether you stand, sit or are otherwise occupied, always make sure that your navel points slightly upward.

This concludes the study of Karate. It is important to realize that the pointers on these pages have emphasized that Karate is not purely a test of physical strength, but that—like Judo, Aikido and other Japanese contest arts—it imbues you with an inner equanimity.

It is to be hoped that every Karateka will devote himself as intensively and selflessly to the mental-spiritual side of the sport as to its techniques, because only by relying on every facet of Karate can you fully benefit from it.

POSITIONS AND MOVEMENTS TO LEARN

Stances

Uchi-hachiji-dachi

Sanchin-dachi

Kake-dachi

Hand techniques

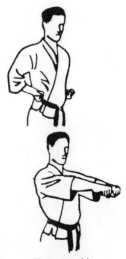

Morote-tsuki

Ura-tsuki

Hand techniques (continued)

Mawashi-tsuki

Tate-tsuki

Yama-tsuki

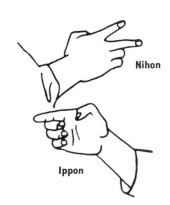

Nihon

Ippon

Strike techniques

Uraken-uchi, downwards

Uraken-uchi, sidewards

138

Koken

Shotei

Wrist snap, downwards and upwards

Koken-uchi

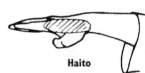

Haito

Shotei-uchi

Haito-uchi, from out in

Haito-uchi, from in out

Foot techniques

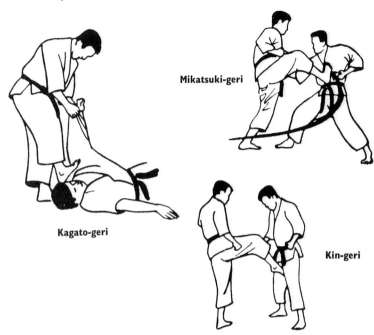

Mikatsuki-geri

Kagato-geri

Kin-geri

Arm defences

Koken-uke

Shotei-uke

Juji-uke defence at the gedan (lower) level against a kick attack.

Morote-uke

Use of leg to defend

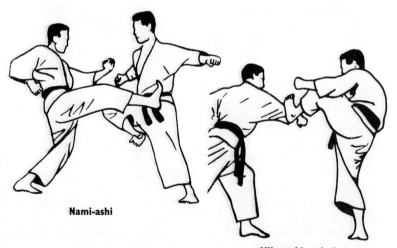

Nami-ashi

Mikatsuki-geri-uke

Index

143